WELCOME TO THE 2017 LEVEL III SCHWESERNOTES™

Thank you for trusting Kaplan Schweser to help you reach your goals. We can help you prepare for the Level III CFA Exam and have done so for many of your predecessors. Level III is well accepted as being different from Levels I and II. That difference leads to exam failure for about half of candidates each year.

When you think of how few candidates reach Level III, the failure rate is shocking, until you accept that the exam is intended to be different. It is half constructed response questions. The purpose of constructed response versus item set questions is to test higher level thinking, judgment, and the ability to organize a response. It differentiates how well candidates know the material. A good constructed response question is one that a high percentage of candidates could answer if shown answer choices A, B, and C but they are unable to answer the same question in constructed response form. The exam is also highly integrated across subjects. If you check the fine print from the CFA Institute, it will tell you that 85–90% is portfolio management. The other 10–15% is ethics and guess what the focus of ethics will be? Portfolio management.

Your previous study skills are useful but generally insufficient for Level III. Let me stress three related things you will need to do. First, finish all the readings, classes, and basic question practice a month before the exam. At Levels I and II, most of you got most of this done just before the exam. Second, spend the last month focused on taking, reviewing, and retaking practice exams. Third, spend a lot of time writing. Buy three new blue or black ink ball point pens. Use them only for writing out answers to practice questions. Wear them out before the exam. We'll return to these three requirements in our material, particularly in the classes.

Basic Preparation

The SchweserNotes™ are the base of our material. Five volumes cover all 18 Study Sessions and every Learning Outcome Statement (LOS). There are examples, Key Concepts, and Concept Checker questions for every reading. At the end of several of the major topic areas, we include a Self-Test. Self-Test questions are created to be exam-like in order to help you evaluate your progress. These SchweserNotes™ provide the base for your preparation and initial practice. **Basic preparation should be complete a month before the exam.**

In addition to basic coverage of the material and practice questions there are:
(1) Professor's Notes with tips to help you learn a topic, concept, or particularly difficult calculation; (2) For the Exam notes with suggestions on how to study for the exam; (3) Warm-Up sections with necessary background material not directly found in the Level III curriculum.

Study Planning

To be successful, you need a **study plan**. The simplest approach is to divide the material so you read and practice each week, finishing the material and allowing a month for intense review. Our classes are a good way to provide structure to your plan. A good study plan includes the following.

- **Complete initial reading and question practice approximately a month before the exam.**
  - **Initial reading of SchweserNotes™ and/or CFA readings.**
  - Complete practice questions in our SchweserNotes™, discussion questions in our ClassNotes, and SchweserPro™ QBank questions. **Work questions every week** or time can get away from you.
  - Complete additional end-of-chapter questions in the CFA readings as time allows.
  - Periodically review previous sessions.
- **Use your last month of study** for final prep and performance.
  - **Complete and review all Schweser practice exams.**
  - **Do the same with the last three years of CFA morning exam sessions and other practice exams** from the CFA Institute.
  - Review material where needed and as indicated by performance on the above.
- **Use the last 7 to 10 days to retake practice exams** to solidify skills (particularly in constructed response) and verify that you can successfully perform what you know.

Those of you who want a more detailed day-by-day study plan can use the **Schweser Study Calendar** to construct one.

We also have a range of other resources available. You can find more details at Schweser .com; just sign in using the individual username and password you received when you purchased the SchweserNotes™. I'll highlight a few below:

Weekly Classes

Live Weekly Classroom Programs   We offer weekly classroom programs around the world. Please check Schweser.com for locations, dates, and availability. The classes can save you time by directing you where to focus in each reading and provide additional questions to work during and after class.

Both the live and online class candidates receive a **weekly class letter** that highlights important issues, specific study hints, and possible pitfalls for that week's material. It regularly addresses that key stumbling block: the constructed response questions.

Getting Started

CFA® 2017

Level III CFA® Exam

Welcome

As the VP of Advanced Designations at Kaplan Schweser, I am pleased to have the opportunity to help you prepare for the 2017 CFA® exam. Getting an early start on your study program is important for you to sufficiently **prepare**, **practice**, and **perform** on exam day. Proper planning will allow you to set aside enough time to master the Learning Outcome Statements (LOS) in the Level III curriculum.

Now that you've received your SchweserNotes™, here's how to get started:

Step 1: Access Your Online Tools

Visit www.schweser.com and log in to your online account using the button located in the top navigation bar. After logging in, select the appropriate level and proceed to the dashboard where you can access your online products.

Step 2: Create a Study Plan

Create a study plan with the **Study Calendar** (located on the Schweser dashboard) and familiarize yourself with your financial calculator. Check out our calculator videos in the **Candidate Resource Library** (also found on the dashboard).

Step 3: Prepare and Practice

Read your SchweserNotes™ Volumes 1–5

At the end of each reading, you can answer the Concept Checker questions for better understanding of the curriculum.

Attend a Weekly Class

Attend live classes online or take part in our live classroom courses in select cities around the world. Our expert faculty will guide you through the curriculum with a structured approach to help you prepare for the CFA® exam. The Schweser On-Demand Video Lectures, in combination with the **Weekly Class**, offer a blended learning approach that covers every LOS in the CFA curriculum. (See our instruction packages to the right. Visit **www.schweser.com/cfa** to order.)

Practice with SchweserPro™ QBank

Maximize your retention of important concepts by answering questions in the **SchweserPro™** QBank and taking several **Practice Exams**. Use Schweser's **Quick Sheet** for continuous review on the go. (Visit **www.schweser.com/cfa** to order.)

Step 4: Attend a 3-Day, 5-Day, or WindsorWeek™ Review Workshop

Schweser's late-season review workshops are designed to drive home the CFA® material, which is critical for CFA exam success. Review key concepts in every topic, **perform** by working through demonstration problems, and **practice** your exam techniques. (See review options to the right.)

Step 5: Perform

Take a **Live** or **Live Online Schweser Mock Exam** to ensure you are ready to **perform** on the actual CFA® exam. Put your skills and knowledge to the test and gain confidence before the exam. (See exam options to the right.)

Again, thank you for trusting Kaplan Schweser with your CFA exam preparation!

Sincerely,

Tim Smaby

Tim Smaby, PhD, CFA, FRM
Vice President, Advanced Designations, Kaplan Schweser

The Kaplan Way for Learning

PREPARE

Acquire new knowledge through demonstration and examples.

PRACTICE

Apply new knowledge through simulation and practice.

PERFORM

Evaluate mastery of new knowledge and identify achieved outcomes.

CFA® Instruction Packages:
> **Premium Instruction Package**
> **PremiumPlus™ Package**

Final Review Options:
> **Live 3-Day Review Workshop** (held in select cities)
> **Live Online 3-Day Review Workshop**
> **NYC 5-Day Review Workshop**
> **DFW 5-Day Review Workshop***
> **WindsorWeek™***
> **Live Schweser Mock Exam** (offered in select cities worldwide)
> **Live Online Schweser Mock Exam**

*Only offered for June exam

Contact us for questions about your study package, upgrading your package, purchasing additional study materials, or for additional information:

888.325.5072 (U.S.) | +1 608.779.8327 (Int'l.)

staff@schweser.com | www.schweser.com/cfa

CFA-536505

BOOK 1 – ETHICAL AND PROFESSIONAL STANDARDS AND BEHAVIORAL FINANCE

SCHWESERNOTES™ 2017 LEVEL III CFA® BOOK 1: ETHICAL AND PROFESSIONAL STANDARDS AND BEHAVIORAL FINANCE

©2016 Kaplan, Inc. All rights reserved.

Published in 2016 by Kaplan, Inc.

Printed in the United States of America.

ISBN: 978-1-4754-4098-0

15-Week Online Classes   Our Live Online Weekly Classes can be watched live and are archived after each class for viewing and review at any time. The tentative schedule is:

Class #	Class #
1) Behavioral Finance and How to Study Ethics; SS1, 2, 3	9) Fixed Income; SS10
2) PM—Individuals; SS4	10) Fixed Income and Equity; SS11, 12
3) PM—Individuals; SS4, 5	11) Alternative Investments and Risk Management; SS13, 14
4) PM—Individuals and Institutional; SS5, 6	12) Risk Management and Derivatives; SS14, 15
5) PM Institutional and Applied Economics; SS6, 7	13) Derivatives; SS15
6) Applied Economics; SS7	14) Trading, Monitoring, and Rebalancing; SS16
7) Asset Allocation 1; SS8	15) Evaluation, How to Study GIPS, and Exam Tips; SS17, 18
8) Asset Allocation 2; SS9	

Class time focuses on key issues in each topic area and applied problem solving of questions. Candidates who wish for more background also have our **On-Demand Video Lectures** that provide more basic LOS-by-LOS coverage.

Ask Your Instructor   In addition to your classroom instructor, Kurt Schuldes, CFA, CAIA, and I can answer questions about the curriculum.

Late Season Preparation

The material discussed above is intended for basic preparation and initial practice. The last month should focus on practice exams with intense review, practice, and performance.

Multi-day Review Workshops   These pull together the material and focus on problem solving with additional questions. Our most complete late-season review courses are residence programs in Windsor, Ontario (WindsorWeek), Dallas/Fort Worth, Texas (DFW five-day program), and the New York five-day program. We also offer three-day Exam Workshops in many cities (and online) that combine curriculum review and hands-on practice with hundreds of questions plus problem-solving techniques. Please check Schweser.com for locations, dates, and availability.

Mock Exam and Multimedia Tutorial   The Schweser Mock Exam is offered live in many cities around the world and online as well. The optional Multimedia Tutorial provides extended explanation and topic tutorials to get you exam-ready in areas where you missed questions on the Mock Exam. Please check Schweser.com for locations, dates, and availability.

Practice Exams We have two volumes with three, full six-hour exams in each. In addition to the answers, we discuss how points are allocated for each constructed response question.

Past Exam Questions The CFA old exam questions for the morning session of the exam are released and are part of your final review. We provide videos for each question with a full review, solution approach, and pitfalls to avoid. But, be careful to not over-rely on the old questions. They are only a sample of what can be asked, so combine them with our practice exams.

Schweser's Secret Sauce® One brief volume highlights key material. It will not replace the full SchweserNotes™ and classes but it is a great review tool for the last month.

How to Succeed

There are no shortcuts. Count on the CFA Institute to think of test angles they have not shown before. Begin your study early and with a plan. Read the SchweserNotes™. Attend a live or online class each week and work practice questions. Take quizzes often using **SchweserPro™ Qbank**. At the end of each topic area, take the Self-Test to check your progress. Review previous topics periodically. Use the CFA texts to supplement weak areas and for additional end-of-chapter questions. Finish this initial study a month before the exam so you have sufficient time to take, review, and retake Practice Exams.

I would like to thank Kurt Schuldes, CFA, CAIA, and Level III content specialist; and Jared Heintz, production project manager; for their contributions to the 2017 Level III SchweserNotes™ for the CFA Exam.

Time to hit the books,

David Hetherington

David Hetherington, CFA
VP and Level III CFA manager

Kaplan Schweser

Exam Topic Weights

1.	Ethical and Professional Standards	10–15%
2.	Economics	5–15%
3.	Fixed Income	10–20%
4.	Equity	5–15%
5.	Alternative Investments	5–15%
6.	Derivatives	5–15%
7.	Portfolio Management and Wealth Planning (This covers all topics not listed above and includes Behavioral Finance, Individual and Institutional Portfolio Management, Asset Allocation, Trading, Evaluation, and GIPS.)	40–55%

The CFA Institute has indicated that these are **guidelines only** and not specific rules they must follow. They have also indicated that **all topics except ethics can be integrated into portfolio management questions.** The most accurate interpretation of Level III is that it is 100% portfolio management.

Exam Format

The morning and afternoon of the exam use different exam formats. Each is three hours long. Both have a maximum score of 180 points out of the total maximum exam score of 360 points.

The morning exam is three hours of constructed response questions. Usually there are 8 to 12 questions with each question having multiple parts. For each question part, you will be directed to answer on either lined paper or in a template. Both the paper and templates are provided in the question book. If you do not answer where directed, you will receive no score for that question part. The morning is usually heavily devoted to portfolio management questions. Every question will state a specified number of minutes. The minutes are the max score you can receive for that question. Most questions do not have one specific right answer but a range of acceptable versus unacceptable answers. Partial credit for an answer is normal.

The afternoon is the multiple choice, item set style of question from Level II. It's three hours for 10 six-question vignettes. Ten times six is 60 individual questions and each has a score of three points. For each question there is one correct answer: A, B, or C.

READINGS AND LEARNING OUTCOME STATEMENTS

READINGS

The following material is a review of the Ethical and Professional Standards and Behavioral Finance principles designed to address the learning outcome statements set forth by CFA Institute.

STUDY SESSION 1

Reading Assignments
Code of Ethics and Standards of Professional Conduct, CFA Program 2017 Curriculum, Volume 1, Level III

STUDY SESSION 2

Reading Assignments
Ethical and Professional Standards in Practice, CFA Program 2017 Curriculum, Volume 1, Level III

STUDY SESSION 3

Reading Assignments
Behavioral Finance, CFA Program 2017 Curriculum, Volume 2, Level III

LEARNING OUTCOME STATEMENTS (LOS)

The CFA Institute learning outcome statements are listed in the following outline. These are repeated in each topic review. However, the order may have been changed in order to get a better fit with the flow of the review.

STUDY SESSION 1

The topical coverage corresponds with the following CFA Institute assigned reading:
1. **Code of Ethics and Standards of Professional Conduct**
   The candidate should be able to:
   a. describe the structure of the CFA Institute Professional Conduct Program and the disciplinary review process for the enforcement of the Code of Ethics and Standards of Professional Conduct. (page 1)
   b. explain the ethical responsibilities required by the Code of Ethics and the Standards of Professional Conduct, including the sub-sections of each standard. (page 2)

The topical coverage corresponds with the following CFA Institute assigned reading:
2. **Guidance for Standards I–VII**
   The candidate should be able to:
   a. demonstrate a thorough knowledge of the Code of Ethics and Standards of Professional Conduct by interpreting the Code and Standards in various situations involving issues of professional integrity. (page 6)
   b. recommend practices and procedures designed to prevent violations of the Code of Ethics and Standards of Professional Conduct. (page 6)

STUDY SESSION 2

The topical coverage corresponds with the following CFA Institute assigned reading:
3. **Application of the Code and Standards**
   The candidate should be able to:
   a. evaluate professional conduct and formulate an appropriate response to actions that violate the Code of Ethics and Standards of Professional Conduct. (page 37)
   b. formulate appropriate policy and procedural changes needed to assure compliance with the Code of Ethics and Standards of Professional Conduct. (page 37)

The topical coverage corresponds with the following CFA Institute assigned reading:
4. **Asset Manager Code of Professional Conduct**
   The candidate should be able to:
   a. explain the purpose of the Asset Manager Code and the benefits that may accrue to a firm that adopts the Code. (page 48)
   b. explain the ethical and professional responsibilities required by the six General Principles of Conduct of the Asset Manager Code. (page 48)
   c. determine whether an asset manager's practices and procedures are consistent with the Asset Manager Code. (page 48)
   d. recommend practices and procedures designed to prevent violations of the Asset Manager Code. (page 48)

STUDY SESSION 3

The topical coverage corresponds with the following CFA Institute assigned reading:

5. **The Behavioral Finance Perspective**

The candidate should be able to:

a. contrast traditional and behavioral finance perspectives on investor decision making. (page 61)

b. contrast expected utility and prospect theories of investment decision making. (page 66)

c. discuss the effect that cognitive limitations and bounded rationality may have on investment decision making. (page 68)

d. compare traditional and behavioral finance perspectives on portfolio construction and the behavior of capital markets. (page 74)

The topical coverage corresponds with the following CFA Institute assigned reading:

6. **The Behavioral Biases of Individuals**

The candidate should be able to:

a. distinguish between cognitive errors and emotional biases. (page 90)

b. discuss commonly recognized behavioral biases and their implications for financial decision making. (page 91)

c. identify and evaluate an individual's behavioral biases. (page 91)

d. evaluate how behavioral biases affect investment policy and asset allocation decisions and recommend approaches to mitigate their effects. (page 91)

The topical coverage corresponds with the following CFA Institute assigned reading:

7. **Behavioral Finance and Investment Processes**

The candidate should be able to:

a. explain the uses and limitations of classifying investors into personality types. (page 110)

b. discuss how behavioral factors affect adviser–client interactions. (page 115)

c. discuss how behavioral factors influence portfolio construction. (page 116)

d. explain how behavioral finance can be applied to the process of portfolio construction. (page 117)

e. discuss how behavioral factors affect analyst forecasts and recommend remedial actions for analyst biases. (page 118)

f. discuss how behavioral factors affect investment committee decision making and recommend techniques for mitigating their effects. (page 121)

g. describe how behavioral biases of investors can lead to market characteristics that may not be explained by traditional finance. (page 122)

CFA INSTITUTE CODE OF ETHICS AND STANDARDS OF PROFESSIONAL CONDUCT GUIDANCE FOR STANDARDS I–VII

Study Session 1

EXAM FOCUS

Ethics will be 10 to 15% of the exam with two or three item set questions. Constructed response questions are also possible this year. Level III questions tend to focus on compliance, portfolio management issues, and questions on the Asset Manager Code. Prepare properly and ethics can be an easier section of the exam. That is a big advantage when you move to the questions in other topic areas.

Just like Level I and Level II, ethics requires that you know the principles and be able to apply them to specific situations to make the expected decision. Some ethics questions can be vague with unclear facts so be prepared to make a "best guess" on a few of the questions. As you read the material, pay particular attention to the numerous examples (the application). As soon as you read, work the Schweser and CFA end of chapter questions. Reading principles without practice questions for application or vice versa will not be sufficient. You need both.

Be prepared and make this an easier part of the exam.

LOS 1.a: Describe the structure of the CFA Institute Professional Conduct Program and the disciplinary review process for the enforcement of the Code of Ethics and Standards of Professional Conduct.

The CFA Institute Professional Conduct Program is covered by the CFA Institute Bylaws and the Rules of Procedure for Proceedings Related to Professional Conduct. The Program is based on the principles of fairness of the process to members and candidates and maintaining the confidentiality of the proceedings. The Disciplinary Review Committee of the CFA Institute Board of Governors has overall responsibility for the Professional Conduct Program and enforcement of the Code and Standards.

The CFA Institute Professional Conduct staff conducts inquiries related to professional conduct. Several circumstances can prompt such an inquiry:

1. Self-disclosure by members or candidates on their annual Professional Conduct Statements of involvement in civil litigation or a criminal investigation, or that the member or candidate is the subject of a written complaint.

2. Written complaints about a member or candidate's professional conduct that are received by the Professional Conduct staff.

3. Evidence of misconduct by a member or candidate that the Professional Conduct staff received through public sources, such as a media article or broadcast.

4. A report by a CFA exam proctor of a possible violation during the examination.

5. Analysis of exam materials and monitoring of social media by CFA Institute.

Once an inquiry has begun, the Professional Conduct staff may request (in writing) an explanation from the subject member or candidate and may: (1) interview the subject member or candidate, (2) interview the complainant or other third parties, and/or (3) collect documents and records relevant to the investigation.

The Professional Conduct staff may decide: (1) that no disciplinary sanctions are appropriate, (2) to issue a cautionary letter, or (3) to discipline the member or candidate. In a case where the Professional Conduct staff finds a violation has occurred and proposes a disciplinary sanction, the member or candidate may accept or reject the sanction. If the member or candidate chooses to reject the sanction, the matter will be referred to a disciplinary review panel of CFA Institute members for a hearing. Sanctions imposed may include condemnation by the member's peers or suspension of candidate's continued participation in the CFA Program.

LOS 1.b: Explain the ethical responsibilities required by the Code of Ethics and the Standards of Professional Conduct, including the sub-sections of each standard.

CODE OF ETHICS

Members of CFA Institute [including Chartered Financial Analyst® (CFA®) charterholders] and candidates for the CFA designation ("Members and Candidates") must:[1]

- Act with integrity, competence, diligence, respect, and in an ethical manner with the public, clients, prospective clients, employers, employees, colleagues in the investment profession, and other participants in the global capital markets.
- Place the integrity of the investment profession and the interests of clients above their own personal interests.
- Use reasonable care and exercise independent professional judgment when conducting investment analysis, making investment recommendations, taking investment actions, and engaging in other professional activities.
- Practice and encourage others to practice in a professional and ethical manner that will reflect credit on themselves and the profession.

- Promote the integrity and viability of the global capital markets for the ultimate benefit of society.
- Maintain and improve their professional competence and strive to maintain and improve the competence of other investment professionals.

THE STANDARDS OF PROFESSIONAL CONDUCT

- I: Professionalism
- II: Integrity of Capital Markets
- III: Duties to Clients
- IV: Duties to Employers
- V: Investment Analysis, Recommendations, and Actions
- VI: Conflicts of Interest
- VII: Responsibilities as a CFA Institute Member or CFA Candidate

STANDARDS OF PROFESSIONAL CONDUCT[2]

I. PROFESSIONALISM

A. Knowledge of the Law. Members and Candidates must understand and comply with all applicable laws, rules, and regulations (including the CFA Institute *Code of Ethics* and *Standards of Professional Conduct*) of any government, regulatory organization, licensing agency, or professional association governing their professional activities. In the event of conflict, Members and Candidates must comply with the more strict law, rule, or regulation. Members and Candidates must not knowingly participate or assist in any violation of laws, rules, or regulations and must disassociate themselves from any such violation.

B. Independence and Objectivity. Members and Candidates must use reasonable care and judgment to achieve and maintain independence and objectivity in their professional activities. Members and Candidates must not offer, solicit, or accept any gift, benefit, compensation, or consideration that reasonably could be expected to compromise their own or another's independence and objectivity.

C. Misrepresentation. Members and Candidates must not knowingly make any misrepresentations relating to investment analysis, recommendations, actions, or other professional activities.

D. Misconduct. Members and Candidates must not engage in any professional conduct involving dishonesty, fraud, or deceit or commit any act that reflects adversely on their professional reputation, integrity, or competence.

II. INTEGRITY OF CAPITAL MARKETS

A. Material Nonpublic Information. Members and Candidates who possess material nonpublic information that could affect the value of an investment must not act or cause others to act on the information.

B. Market Manipulation. Members and Candidates must not engage in practices that distort prices or artificially inflate trading volume with the intent to mislead market participants.

---

2.   Ibid.

III.   DUTIES TO CLIENTS

A. **Loyalty, Prudence, and Care.** Members and Candidates have a duty of loyalty to their clients and must act with reasonable care and exercise prudent judgment. Members and Candidates must act for the benefit of their clients and place their clients' interests before their employer's or their own interests.

B. **Fair Dealing.** Members and Candidates must deal fairly and objectively with all clients when providing investment analysis, making investment recommendations, taking investment action, or engaging in other professional activities.

C. **Suitability.**

1. When Members and Candidates are in an advisory relationship with a client, they must:

a.   Make a reasonable inquiry into a client's or prospective clients' investment experience, risk and return objectives, and financial constraints prior to making any investment recommendation or taking investment action and must reassess and update this information regularly.

b.   Determine that an investment is suitable to the client's financial situation and consistent with the client's written objectives, mandates, and constraints before making an investment recommendation or taking investment action.

c.   Judge the suitability of investments in the context of the client's total portfolio.

2. When Members and Candidates are responsible for managing a portfolio to a specific mandate, strategy, or style, they must make only investment recommendations or take investment actions that are consistent with the stated objectives and constraints of the portfolio.

D. **Performance Presentation.** When communicating investment performance information, Members or Candidates must make reasonable efforts to ensure that it is fair, accurate, and complete.

E. **Preservation of Confidentiality.** Members and Candidates must keep information about current, former, and prospective clients confidential unless:

1. The information concerns illegal activities on the part of the client or prospective client,

2. Disclosure is required by law, or

3. The client or prospective client permits disclosure of the information.

IV.   DUTIES TO EMPLOYERS

   A.   **Loyalty.** In matters related to their employment, Members and Candidates must act for the benefit of their employer and not deprive their employer of the advantage of their skills and abilities, divulge confidential information, or otherwise cause harm to their employer.

   B.   **Additional Compensation Arrangements.** Members and Candidates must not accept gifts, benefits, compensation, or consideration that competes with, or might reasonably be expected to create a conflict of interest with, their employer's interest unless they obtain written consent from all parties involved.

   C.   **Responsibilities of Supervisors.** Members and Candidates must make reasonable efforts to ensure that anyone subject to their supervision or authority complies with applicable laws, rules, regulations, and the Code and Standards.

V.   INVESTMENT ANALYSIS, RECOMMENDATIONS, AND ACTIONS

   A.   **Diligence and Reasonable Basis.** Members and Candidates must:

      1.   Exercise diligence, independence, and thoroughness in analyzing investments, making investment recommendations, and taking investment actions.

      2.   Have a reasonable and adequate basis, supported by appropriate research and investigation, for any investment analysis, recommendation, or action.

   B.   **Communication with Clients and Prospective Clients.** Members and Candidates must:

      1.   Disclose to clients and prospective clients the basic format and general principles of the investment processes used to analyze investments, select securities, and construct portfolios and must promptly disclose any changes that might materially affect those processes.

      2.   Disclose to clients and prospective clients significant limitations and risks associated with the investment process.

      3.   Use reasonable judgment in identifying which factors are important to their investment analyses, recommendations, or actions and include those factors in communications with clients and prospective clients.

      4.   Distinguish between fact and opinion in the presentation of investment analysis and recommendations.

   C.   **Record Retention.** Members and Candidates must develop and maintain appropriate records to support their investment analysis, recommendations, actions, and other investment-related communications with clients and prospective clients.

VI. CONFLICTS OF INTEREST

A. **Disclosure of Conflicts.** Members and Candidates must make full and fair disclosure of all matters that could reasonably be expected to impair their independence and objectivity or interfere with respective duties to their clients, prospective clients, and employer. Members and Candidates must ensure that such disclosures are prominent, are delivered in plain language, and communicate the relevant information effectively.

B. **Priority of Transactions.** Investment transactions for clients and employers must have priority over investment transactions in which a Member or Candidate is the beneficial owner.

C. **Referral Fees.** Members and Candidates must disclose to their employer, clients, and prospective clients, as appropriate, any compensation, consideration, or benefit received from, or paid to, others for the recommendation of products or services.

VII. RESPONSIBILITIES AS A CFA INSTITUTE MEMBER OR CFA CANDIDATE

A. **Conduct as Participants in CFA Institute Programs.** Members and Candidates must not engage in any conduct that compromises the reputation or integrity of CFA Institute or the CFA designation or the integrity, validity, or security of CFA Institute programs.

B. **Reference to CFA Institute, the CFA Designation, and the CFA Program.** When referring to CFA Institute, CFA Institute membership, the CFA designation, or candidacy in the CFA Program, Members and Candidates must not misrepresent or exaggerate the meaning or implications of membership in CFA Institute, holding the CFA designation, or candidacy in the CFA Program.

LOS 2.a: Demonstrate a thorough knowledge of the Code of Ethics and Standards of Professional Conduct by interpreting the Code and Standards in various situations involving issues of professional integrity.

LOS 2.b: Recommend practices and procedures designed to prevent violations of the Code of Ethics and Standards of Professional Conduct.

Professor's Note: You should be prepared for questions that require you to apply the Standards in specific case situations. In such questions, you must recognize the case facts described and then decide which Standards are directly relevant. This is primarily a test of critical thinking, not of memorization. To prepare you, we will in this section focus on a review of the key points for each Standard and the recommended procedures. If you know the main issues, you are more likely to successfully apply them. You should review the recommended procedures several times between now and exam day because they fit the Level III emphasis on the bigger picture and managing the business as well as portfolios and assets. Once you complete our review and understand the basic principals that you must know, then move to application and practice. For practice, complete our sample questions. The CFA reading includes many examples of applying the Standards, and you should read all the examples as well as complete the CFA end of chapter questions for this reading.

It is important you know the basic principals before you move to the specific examples and questions. Those examples and question can only be a sample of possible applications. When you try to learn by practice only, without first knowing the principals that are being applied, you generally get the wrong ideas. Prepare and practice are two different steps. The combination is what leads to success. Do both.

In many cases the actions that members and candidates must not take are explained using terms open to interpretation, such as "reasonable," "adequate," and "token."

Some examples from the Standards themselves are:
…use reasonable care and judgment to achieve…
…accept any gift, that reasonably could be expected to compromise…
…act with reasonable care and exercise prudent judgment…
…deal fairly and objectively with all clients…
…make a reasonable inquiry into…
…make reasonable efforts to ensure…
…might reasonably be expected to create a conflict of interest with…
…Have a reasonable and adequate basis…
…Use reasonable judgment in…
…matters that could be reasonably expected to impair…

The requirement of the LOS is that you know what constitutes a violation, not that you draw a distinction between what is "reasonable" and what is not in a given situation. We believe the exam writers take this into account and that if they intend, for example, to test whether a recommendation has been given without reasonable care and judgment, it will likely be clear either that the care and judgment exhibited by the analyst did not rise to the level of "reasonable," or that it did.

No monetary value for a "token" gift is given in the Standards, although it is recommended that a firm establish such a monetary value for its employees. Here, again, the correct answer to a question will not likely hinge on candidate's determination of what is a token gift and what is not. Questions should be clear in this regard. A business dinner is likely a token gift, but a week at a condominium in Aspen or tickets to the

Super Bowl are likely not. Always look for clues in the questions that lead you to the question-writer's preferred answer choice, such as "lavish" entertainment and "luxury" accommodations.

Below, we present a summary of each subsection of the Standards of Professional Conduct. For each one, we first detail actions that violate the Standard and then list actions and behaviors that are recommended within the Standards. We suggest you learn the violations especially well so you understand that the other items are recommended. For the exam, it is not necessary to memorize the Standard number and subsection letter. Knowing that an action violates, for example, Professionalism, rather than Duties to Employers or Duties to Clients, should be sufficient in this regard. Note that some actions may violate more than one Standard.

One way to write questions for this material is to offer a reason that might make one believe a Standard does not apply in a particular situation. In most, if not all, cases the "reason" does not change the requirement of the Standard. If you are prohibited from some action, the motivations for the action or other circumstances simply do not matter. If the Standard says it's a violation, it's a violation. An exception is when intent is key to the Standard, such as intending to mislead clients or market participants in general.

STANDARD I: PROFESSIONALISM[3]

Standard I(A) Knowledge of the Law

Members and Candidates must understand and comply with all applicable laws, rules, and regulations (including the CFA Institute Code of Ethics and Standards of Professional Conduct) of any government, regulatory organization, licensing agency, or professional association governing their professional activities. In the event of conflict, Members and Candidates must comply with the more strict law, rule, or regulation. Members and Candidates must not knowingly participate or assist in and must dissociate from any violation of such laws, rules, or regulations.

The Standards begin with a straightforward statement: Don't violate any laws, rules, or regulations that apply to your professional activities. This includes the Code and Standards, so any violation of the Code and Standards will also violate this subsection.

A member may be governed by different rules and regulations among the Standards, the country in which the member resides, and the country where the member is doing business. Follow the most strict of these, or, put another way, do not violate any of the three sets of rules and regulations.

If you know that violations of applicable rules or laws are taking place, either by coworkers or clients, you must approach your supervisor or compliance department to remedy the situation. If they will not or cannot, then you must dissociate from the activity (e.g., not working with a trading group you know is not allocating client

---

3   Copyright 2014, CFA Institute. Reproduced and republished from "The Code of Ethics," from *Standards of Practice Handbook, 11th Ed.*, 2014, with permission from CFA Institute. All rights reserved.

trades properly according to the Standard on Fair Dealing, or not using marketing materials that you know or should know are misleading or erroneous). If this cannot be accomplished, you may, in an extreme case, have to resign from the firm to be in compliance with this Standard.

Recommendations for Members

- Establish, or encourage employer to establish, procedures to keep employees informed of changes in relevant laws, rules, and regulations.
- Review, or encourage employer to review, the firm's written compliance procedures on a regular basis.
- Maintain, or encourage employer to maintain, copies of current laws, rules, and regulations.
- When in doubt about legality, consult supervisor, compliance personnel, or a lawyer.
- When dissociating from violations, keep records documenting the violations, encourage employer to bring an end to the violations.
- There is no requirement in the Standards to report wrongdoers, but local law may require it; members are "strongly encouraged" to report violations to CFA Institute Professional Conduct Program.

Recommendations for Firms

- Have a code of ethics.
- Provide employees with information on laws, rules, and regulations governing professional activities.
- Have procedures for reporting suspected violations.

Standard I(B) Independence and Objectivity

Members and Candidates must use reasonable care and judgment to achieve and maintain independence and objectivity in their professional activities. Members and Candidates must not offer, solicit, or accept any gift, benefit, compensation, or consideration that reasonably could be expected to compromise their own or another's independence and objectivity.

Analysts may face pressure or receive inducements to give a security a specific rating, to select certain outside managers or vendors, or to produce favorable or unfavorable research and conclusions. Members who allow their investment recommendations or analysis to be influenced by such pressure or inducements will have violated the requirement to use reasonable care and to maintain independence and objectivity in their professional activities. Allocating shares in oversubscribed IPOs to personal accounts is a violation.

Normal business entertainment is permitted. Members who accept, solicit, or offer things of value that could be expected to influence the member's or others' independence or objectivity are violating the Standard. Gifts from clients are considered less likely to compromise independence and objectivity than gifts from other parties. Client gifts must be disclosed to the member's employer prior to acceptance, if possible, but after acceptance, if not.

Members may prepare reports paid for by the subject firm if compensation is a flat rate not tied to the conclusions of the report (and if the fact that the research is issuer-paid is disclosed). Accepting compensation that is dependent on the conclusions, recommendations, or market impact of the report, and failure to disclose that research is issuer-paid, are violations of this Standard.

Recommendations for Members

Members or their firms should pay for their own travel to company events or tours when practicable and limit use of corporate aircraft to trips for which commercial travel is not an alternative.

Recommendations for Firms

- Establish policies requiring every research report to reflect the unbiased opinion of the analyst and align compensation plans to support this principal.
- Establish and review written policies and procedures to assure research is independent and objective.
- Establish restricted lists of securities for which the firm is not willing to issue adverse opinions. Factual information may still be provided.
- Limit gifts from non-clients to token amounts.
- Limit and require prior approval of employee participation in equity IPOs.
- Establish procedures for supervisory review of employee actions.
- Appoint a senior officer to oversee firm compliance and ethics.

Standard I(C) Misrepresentation

Members and Candidates must not knowingly make any misrepresentations relating to investment analysis, recommendations, actions, or other professional activities.

Misrepresentation includes knowingly misleading investors, omitting relevant information, presenting selective data to mislead investors, and plagiarism. Plagiarism is using reports, forecasts, models, ideas, charts, graphs, or spreadsheets created by others without crediting the source. Crediting the source is not required when using projections, statistics, and tables from recognized financial and statistical reporting services. When using models developed or research done by other members of the firm, it is permitted to omit the names of those who are no longer with the firm as long as the member does not represent work previously done by others as his alone.

Actions that would violate the Standard include:

- Presenting third-party research as your own, without attribution to the source.
- Guaranteeing a specific return on securities that do not have an explicit guarantee from a government body or financial institution.
- Selecting a valuation service because it puts the highest value on untraded security holdings.
- Selecting a performance benchmark that is not comparable to the investment strategy employed.

- Presenting performance data or attribution analysis that omits accounts or relevant variables.
- Offering false or misleading information about the analyst's or firm's capabilities, expertise, or experience.
- Using marketing materials from a third party (outside advisor) that are misleading.

Recommendations for Members

- Understand the scope and limits of the firm's capabilities to avoid inadvertent misrepresentations.
- Summarize your own qualifications and experience.
- Make reasonable efforts to verify information from third parties that is provided to clients.
- Regularly maintain webpages for accuracy.
- Avoid plagiarism by keeping copies of all research reports and supporting documents and attributing direct quotes, paraphrases, and summaries to their source.

Standard I(D) Misconduct

Members and Candidates must not engage in any professional conduct involving dishonesty, fraud, or deceit or commit any act that reflects adversely on their professional reputation, integrity, or competence.

The first part here regarding professional conduct is clear: no dishonesty, fraud, or deceit. The second part, while it applies to all conduct by the member, specifically requires that the act, "reflects adversely on their professional reputation, integrity, or competence." The guidance states, in fact, that members must not try to use enforcement of this Standard against another member to settle personal, political, or other disputes that are not related to professional ethics or competence.

Recommendations for Firms

- Develop and adopt a code of ethics and make clear that unethical behavior will not be tolerated.
- Give employees a list of potential violations and sanctions, including dismissal.
- Check references of potential employees.

STANDARD II: INTEGRITY OF CAPITAL MARKETS

Standard II(A) Material Nonpublic Information

Members and Candidates who possess material nonpublic information that could affect the value of an investment must not act or cause others to act on the information.

Information is "material" if its disclosure would affect the price of a security or if a reasonable investor would want the information before making an investment decision. Information that is ambiguous as to its likely effect on price may not be considered material.

Information is "nonpublic" until it has been made available to the marketplace. An analyst conference call is not public disclosure. Selective disclosure of information by corporations creates the potential for insider-trading violations.

The prohibition against acting on material nonpublic information extends to mutual funds containing the subject securities as well as related swaps and options contracts. It is the member's responsibility to determine if information she receives has been publicly disseminated prior to acting or causing others to act on it.

Some members and candidates may be involved in transactions during which they are provided with material nonpublic information by firms (e.g., investment banking transactions). Members and candidates may use this information for its intended purpose, but must not use the information for any other purpose unless it becomes public information.

Under the so-called **mosaic theory**, reaching an investment conclusion through perceptive analysis of public information combined with non-material nonpublic information is not a violation of the Standard.

Recommendations for Members

- Make reasonable efforts to achieve public dissemination by the firm of information they possess.
- Encourage their firms to adopt procedures to prevent the misuse of material nonpublic information.

Recommendations for Firms

- Issue press releases prior to analyst meetings to assure public dissemination of any new information.
- Adopt procedures for equitable distribution of information to the market place (e.g., new research opinions and reports to clients).
- Establish firewalls within the organization for who may and may not have access to material nonpublic information. Generally, this includes having the legal or compliance department clear interdepartmental communications, reviewing employee trades, documenting procedures to limit information flow, and carefully reviewing or restricting proprietary trading whenever the firm possesses material nonpublic information on the securities involved.
- Ensure that procedures for proprietary trading are appropriate to the strategies used. A blanket prohibition is not required.
- Develop procedures to enforce firewalls with complexity consistent with the complexity of the firm.
- Physically separate departments.
- Have a compliance (or other) officer review and authorize information flows before sharing.
- Maintain records of information shared.
- Limit personal trading, require that it be reported, and establish a restricted list of securities in which personal trading is not allowed.
- Regularly communicate with and train employees to follow procedures.

Standard II(B) Market Manipulation

Members and Candidates must not engage in practices that distort prices or artificially inflate trading volume with the intent to mislead market participants.

Member actions may affect security values and trading volumes without violating this Standard. The key point here is that if there is the *intent to mislead,* then the Standard is violated. Of course, spreading false information to affect prices or volume is a violation of this Standard as is making trades intended to mislead market participants.

STANDARD III: DUTIES TO CLIENTS

Standard III(A) Loyalty, Prudence, and Care

Members and Candidates have a duty of loyalty to their clients and must act with reasonable care and exercise prudent judgment. Members and Candidates must act for the benefit of their clients and place their clients' interests before their employer's or their own interests.

Client interests always come first. Although this Standard does not impose a fiduciary duty on members or candidates where one did not already exist, it does require members and candidates to act in their clients' best interests and recommend products that are suitable given their clients' investment objectives and risk tolerances. Members and candidates must:

- Exercise the prudence, care, skill, and diligence under the circumstances that a person acting in a like capacity and familiar with such matters would use.
- Manage pools of client assets in accordance with the terms of the governing documents, such as trust documents or investment management agreements.
- Make investment decisions in the context of the total portfolio.
- Inform clients of any limitations in an advisory relationship (e.g., an advisor who may only recommend her own firm's products).
- Vote proxies in an informed and responsible manner. Due to cost-benefit considerations, it may not be necessary to vote all proxies.
- Client brokerage, or "soft dollars" or "soft commissions," must be used to benefit the client.
- The "client" may be the investing public as a whole rather than a specific entity or person.

Recommendations for Members

Submit to clients, at least quarterly, itemized statements showing all securities in custody and all debits, credits, and transactions. Disclose where client assets are held and if they are moved. Keep client assets separate from others' assets.

If in doubt as to the appropriate action, what would you do if you were the client? If still in doubt, disclose and seek written client approval.

Encourage firms to address these topics when drafting policies and procedures regarding fiduciary duty:

- Follow applicable rules and laws.
- Establish investment objectives of client.
- Consider suitability of a portfolio relative to the client's needs and circumstances, the investment's basic characteristics, or the basic characteristics of the total portfolio.
- Diversify unless account guidelines dictate otherwise.
- Deal fairly with all clients in regard to investment actions.
- Disclose conflicts of interest.
- Disclose manager compensation arrangements.
- Regularly review actions for consistency with documents.
- Vote proxies in the best interest of clients and ultimate beneficiaries.
- Maintain confidentiality.
- Seek best execution.
- Put client interests first.

Standard III(B) Fair Dealing

Members and Candidates must deal fairly and objectively with all clients when providing investment analysis, making investment recommendations, taking investment action, or engaging in other professional activities.

Do not discriminate against any clients when disseminating recommendations or taking investment action. "Fairly" does not mean "equally." In the normal course of business, there will be differences in the time emails, faxes, and other communications are received by different clients.

Different service levels are acceptable, but they must not negatively affect or disadvantage any clients. Disclose the different service levels to all clients and prospects, and make premium levels of service available to all those willing to pay for them.

Give all clients a fair opportunity to act on every recommendation. Clients who are unaware of a change in the recommendation for a security should be advised of the change before an order for the security is accepted.

Treat clients fairly in light of their investment objectives and circumstances. Treat both individual and institutional clients in a fair and impartial manner. Members and candidates should not take advantage of their position in the industry to disadvantage clients (e.g., taking shares of an oversubscribed IPO).

Recommendations for Members

- Encourage firms to establish compliance procedures requiring proper dissemination of investment recommendations and fair treatment of all customers and clients.
- Maintain a list of clients and holdings—use to ensure that all holders are treated fairly.

Recommendations for Firms

- Limit the number of people who are aware that a change in recommendation will be made.
- Shorten the time frame between decision and dissemination.
- Publish personnel guidelines for pre-dissemination—have in place guidelines prohibiting personnel who have prior knowledge of a recommendation from discussing it or taking action on the pending recommendation.
- Disseminate new or changed recommendations simultaneously to all clients who have expressed an interest or for whom an investment is suitable.
- Establish systematic account review—ensure that no client is given preferred treatment and that investment actions are consistent with the account's objectives.
- Disclose available levels of service and the associated fees.
- Disclose trade allocation procedures.
- Develop written trade allocation procedures to:
  - Document and time stamp all orders.
  - Bundle orders and then execute on a first come, first fill basis.
  - Allocate partially filled orders.
  - Provide the same net (after costs) execution price to all clients in a block trade.

Standard III(C) Suitability

1. When Members and Candidates are in an advisory relationship with a client, they must:

    a. Make a reasonable inquiry into a client's or prospective client's investment experience, risk and return objectives, and financial constraints prior to making any investment recommendation or taking investment action and must reassess and update this information regularly.

    b. Determine that an investment is suitable to the client's financial situation and consistent with the client's written objectives, mandates, and constraints before making an investment recommendation or taking investment action.

    c. Judge the suitability of investments in the context of the client's total portfolio.

2. When Members and Candidates are responsible for managing a portfolio to a specific mandate, strategy, or style, they must make only investment recommendations or take only investment actions that are consistent with the stated objectives and constraints of the portfolio.

In advisory relationships, members must gather client information at the beginning of the relationship, in the form of an investment policy statement (IPS). Consider clients' needs and circumstances and, thus, their risk tolerance. Consider whether or not the use of leverage is suitable for the client.

If a member is responsible for managing a fund to an index or other stated mandate, he must select only investments that are consistent with the stated mandate.

Unsolicited Trade Requests

An investment manager may receive a client request to purchase a security that the manager knows is unsuitable, given the client's investment policy statement. The trade may or may not have a material effect on the risk characteristics of the client's total portfolio and the requirements are different for each case. In either case, however, the manager should not make the trade until he has discussed with the client the reasons (based on the IPS) that the trade is unsuitable for the client's account.

If the manager determines that the *effect on the risk/return profile of the client's total portfolio is minimal,* the manager, after discussing with the client how the trade does not fit the IPS goals and constraints, may follow his firm's policy with regard to unsuitable trades. Regardless of firm policy, the client must acknowledge the discussion and an understanding of why the trade is unsuitable.

If the trade would have a *material impact on the risk/return profile of the client's total portfolio,* one option is to update the IPS so the client accepts a changed risk profile that would permit the trade. If the client will not accept a changed IPS, the manager may follow firm policy, which may allow the trade to be made in a separate client-directed account. In the absence of other options, the manager may need to reconsider whether to maintain the relationship with the client.

Recommendations for Members
- Establish a written IPS, considering type of client and account beneficiaries, the objectives, constraints, and the portion of the client's assets managed.
- Review the IPS annually and update for material changes in client and market circumstances.
- Develop policies and procedures to assess suitability of portfolio changes. Consider the impact on diversification, risk, and meeting the client's investment strategy.

Standard III(D) Performance Presentation

When communicating investment performance information, Members and Candidates must make reasonable efforts to ensure that it is fair, accurate, and complete.

Members must not misstate performance or mislead clients or prospects about their investment performance or their firm's investment performance.

Members must not misrepresent past performance or reasonably expected performance, and must not state or imply the ability to achieve a rate of return similar to that achieved in the past.

For brief presentations, members must make detailed information available on request and indicate that the presentation has offered only limited information.

Recommendations for Members

- Encourage firms to adhere to Global Investment Performance Standards.
- Consider the sophistication of the audience to whom a performance presentation is addressed.
- Present the performance of a weighted composite of similar portfolios rather than the performance of a single account.
- Include terminated accounts as part of historical performance and clearly state when they were terminated.
- Include all appropriate disclosures to fully explain results (e.g., model results included, gross or net of fees, etc.).
- Maintain data and records used to calculate the performance being presented.

Standard III(E) Preservation of Confidentiality

Members and Candidates must keep information about current, former, and prospective clients confidential unless:

1. The information concerns illegal activities on the part of the client;

2. Disclosure is required by law; or

3. The client or prospective client permits disclosure of the information.

If illegal activities by a client are involved, members may have an obligation to report the activities to authorities.

The confidentiality Standard extends to former clients as well.

The requirements of this Standard are not intended to prevent members and candidates from cooperating with a CFA Institute Professional Conduct Program (PCP) investigation.

Recommendations for Members

- Members should avoid disclosing information received from a client except to authorized coworkers who are also working for the client. Consider whether the disclosure is necessary and will benefit the client.
- Members should follow firm procedures for storage of electronic data and recommend adoption of such procedures if they are not in place.
- Assure client information is not accidentally disclosed.

STANDARD IV: DUTIES TO EMPLOYERS

Standard IV(A) Loyalty

In matters related to their employment, Members and Candidates must act for the benefit of their employer and not deprive their employer of the advantage of their skills and abilities, divulge confidential information, or otherwise cause harm to their employer.

This Standard is applicable to employees. If members are independent contractors, rather than employees, they have a duty to abide by the terms of their agreements.

Members must not engage in any activities that would injure the firm, deprive it of profit, or deprive it of the advantage of employees' skills and abilities.

Members should always place client interests above interests of their employer, but consider the effects of their actions on firm integrity and sustainability.

There is no requirement that the employee put employer interests ahead of family and other personal obligations; it is expected that employers and employees will discuss such matters and balance these obligations with work obligations.

There may be isolated cases where a duty to one's employer may be violated in order to protect clients or the integrity of the market, when the actions are not for personal gain. This may be referred to as whistle-blowing.

Independent practice for compensation is allowed if a notification is provided to the employer fully describing all aspects of the services, including compensation, duration, and the nature of the activities and the employer consents to all terms of the proposed independent practice before it begins.

Professor's Note: The distinction between an employee and contractor is important in applying this and other standards. Think of it as employee status conveys an implication of an exclusive work relationship with the employer and contractor does not. To engage in outside practice or accept additional compensation requires disclosure and approval from the employer. But consider an individual who directly offers services to various clients. The manager is self-employed. With no inference of exclusivity, there is no need to notify or receive approval to add another client. This still leaves other responsibilities in place. If the clients expected or were told the manager is full time self-employed and goes to part time or also becomes an employee at another firm, that is almost certainly material to any reasonable client and must be disclosed.

When leaving an employer, members must continue to act in their employer's best interests until their resignation is effective. Activities that may constitute a violation include:

- Misappropriation of trade secrets.
- Misuse of confidential information.

- Soliciting employer's clients prior to leaving.
- Self-dealing.
- Misappropriation of client lists.

Employer records on any medium (e.g., home computer, tablet, cell phone) are the property of the firm.

When an employee has left a firm, simple knowledge of names and existence of former clients is generally not confidential. There is also no prohibition on the use of experience or knowledge gained while with a former employer. If an agreement exists among employers (e.g., the U.S. "Protocol for Broker Recruiting") that permits brokers to take certain client information when leaving a firm, a member may act within the terms of the agreement without violating the Standard.

Members and candidates must adhere to their employers' policies concerning social media. When planning to leave an employer, members and candidates must ensure that their social media use complies with their employers' policies for notifying clients about employee separations.

Recommendations for Members

- Keep personal and professional social media accounts separate. Business-related accounts approved by the firm constitute employer assets.
- Understand and follow the employer's policies regarding competitive activities, termination of employment, whistleblowing, and whether you are considered a full- or part-time employee, or a contractor.

Recommendations for Firms

Employers should not have incentive and compensation systems that encourage unethical behavior.

- Establish codes of conduct and related procedures.

Standard IV(B) Additional Compensation Arrangements

Members and Candidates must not accept gifts, benefits, compensation, or consideration that competes with or might reasonably be expected to create a conflict of interest with their employer's interest unless they obtain written consent from all parties involved.

Compensation includes direct and indirect compensation from a client and other benefits received from third parties.

Written consent from a member's employer includes email communication.

Understand the difference between an additional compensation arrangement and a gift from a client:

- If a client offers a bonus that depends on the *future performance* of her account, this is an additional compensation arrangement that requires written consent in advance.
- If a client offers a bonus to reward a member for her account's *past performance,* this is a gift that requires disclosure to the member's employer to comply with Standard I(B) Independence and Objectivity.

Recommendations for Members

Make an immediate written report to the employer detailing any proposed compensation and services, if additional to that provided by the employer. It should disclose the nature, approximate amount, and duration of compensation.

Members and candidates who are hired to work part time should discuss any arrangements that may compete with their employer's interest at the time they are hired and abide by any limitations their employer identifies.

Standard IV(C) Responsibilities of Supervisors

Members and Candidates must make reasonable efforts to ensure that anyone subject to their supervision or authority complies with applicable laws, rules, regulations, and the Code and Standards.

Members with employees subject to her control or influence must have in-depth knowledge of the Code and Standards. Those members must make reasonable efforts to prevent employees from violating laws, rules, regulations, or the Code and Standards, as well as make reasonable efforts to detect violations.

An adequate compliance system must meet industry standards, regulatory requirements, and the requirements of the Code and Standards.

Members with supervisory responsibilities have an obligation to bring an inadequate compliance system to the attention of firm's management and recommend corrective action.

A member or candidate faced with no compliance procedures or with procedures he believes are inadequate must decline supervisory responsibility in writing until adequate procedures are adopted by the firm.

Recommendations for Members

A member should recommend that his employer adopt a code of ethics. Members should encourage employers to provide their codes of ethics to clients.

Once the compliance program is instituted, the supervisor should:

- Distribute it to the proper personnel.

- Update it as needed.
- Continually educate staff regarding procedures.
- Issue reminders as necessary.
- Require professional conduct evaluations.
- Review employee actions to monitor compliance and identify violations.
- Respond promptly to violations, investigate thoroughly, increase supervision while investigating the suspected employee, and consider changes to prevent future violations.

Recommendations for Firms

Do not confuse the code with compliance. The code is general principles in plain language. Compliance is detailed procedures to meet the code.

Compliance procedures should:

- Be clearly written.
- Be easy to understand.
- Designate a compliance officer with authority clearly defined.
- Have a system of checks and balances.
- Establish a hierarchy of supervisors.
- Outline the scope of procedures.
- Outline what conduct is permitted.
- Contain procedures for reporting violations and sanctions.

The supervisor must then:

- Disseminate the compliance program to appropriate personnel and periodically update the program.
- Continually educate and remind personnel to follow the program.
- Make professional conduct review part of employee review.
- Review employee actions to identify and then correct violations.

When a violation is detected, the supervisor must:

- Respond promptly and investigate thoroughly.
- Supervise the accused closely until the issue is resolved.
- Consider changes to minimize future violations.

Ethics education will not deter fraud, but when combined with regular compliance training, it will establish an ethical culture and alert employees to potential ethical and legal pitfalls.

Incentive compensation plans must reinforce ethical behavior by designing them to align employee incentives with client best interests (e.g., don't incent inappropriate risk taking or other actions detrimental to the client).

STANDARD V: INVESTMENT ANALYSIS, RECOMMENDATIONS, AND ACTIONS

Standard V(A) Diligence and Reasonable Basis

Members and Candidates must:

1. Exercise diligence, independence, and thoroughness in analyzing investments, making investment recommendations, and taking investment actions.

2. Have a reasonable and adequate basis, supported by appropriate research and investigation, for any investment analysis, recommendation, or action.

The application of this Standard depends on the investment philosophy adhered to, members' and candidates' roles in the investment decision-making process, and the resources and support provided by employers. These factors dictate the degree of diligence, thoroughness of research, and the proper level of investigation required.

The level of research needed to satisfy the requirement for due diligence will differ depending on the product or service offered. A list of things that should be considered prior to making a recommendation or taking investment action includes:

- Global and national economic conditions.
- A firm's financial results and operating history, and the business cycle stage.
- Fees and historical results for a mutual fund.
- Limitations of any quantitative models used.
- A determination of whether peer group comparisons for valuation are appropriate.

Evaluate the quality of third-party research. Examples of criteria to use in judging quality are:

- Review assumptions used.
- Determine how rigorous the analysis was.
- Identify how timely the research is.
- Evaluate objectivity and independence of the recommendations.

When **using** quantitative research such as computer-based models, screens, and rankings, members need not be experts. However, they must understand the basic assumptions and risks and consider a range of input values and the resulting effects on output. When **creating** such models, a higher level of knowledge and understanding is required.

Develop standardized criteria to evaluate external advisors and subadvisors, such as considering:

- The advisors' code of ethics plus their compliance and control procedures.
- The quality of their return information and process to maintain adherence to intended strategy.

When participating in group research or decision making, members who disagree need not dissent or disassociate from the final conclusion, as long as the conclusion was based on a reasonable and adequate basis and was independently and objectively developed.

Recommendations for Members

Members should *encourage their firms to consider* these policies and procedures supporting this Standard:

- Have a policy requiring that research reports and recommendations have a basis that can be substantiated as reasonable and adequate.
- Have detailed, written guidance for proper research, supervision, and due diligence.
- Have measurable criteria for judging the quality of research, and base analyst compensation on such criteria.
- Have written procedures that provide a minimum acceptable level of scenario testing for computer-based models and include standards for the range of scenarios, model accuracy over time, and a measure of the sensitivity of cash flows to model assumptions and inputs.
- Have a policy for evaluating outside providers of information that addresses the reasonableness and accuracy of the information provided and establishes how often the evaluations should be repeated.
- Adopt a set of standards that provides criteria for evaluating external advisers and states how often a review of external advisers will be performed.

Standard V(B) Communication with Clients and Prospective Clients

Members and Candidates must:

1. Disclose to clients and prospective clients the basic format and general principles of the investment processes they use to analyze investments, select securities, and construct portfolios and must promptly disclose any changes that might materially affect those processes.

2. Disclose to clients and prospective clients significant limitations and risks associated with the investment process.

3. Use reasonable judgment in identifying which factors are important to their investment analyses, recommendations, or actions and include those factors in communications with clients and prospective clients.

4. Distinguish between fact and opinion in the presentation of investment analyses and recommendations.

All means and types of communication with clients are covered by this Standard, not just research reports or other written communications.

Members must distinguish between opinions and facts and always include the basic characteristics of the security being analyzed in a research report. Expectations based on statistical modeling and analysis are not facts.

Members must explain to clients and prospects the investment decision-making process used.

In preparing recommendations for structured securities, allocation strategies, or any other nontraditional investment, members must communicate those risk factors specific to such investments.

Members must communicate significant changes in the risk characteristics of an investment or investment strategy.

Members must update clients regularly about any changes in the investment process, including any risks and limitations that have been newly identified.

When using projections from quantitative models and analysis, members may violate the Standard by not explaining the limitations of the model and the assumptions it uses, which provides a context for judging the uncertainty regarding the estimated investment result.

Members and candidates must inform clients about limitations inherent to an investment. Two examples of such limitations are liquidity and capacity. Liquidity refers to the ability to exit an investment readily without experiencing a significant extra cost from doing so. Capacity refers to an investment vehicle's ability to absorb additional investment without reducing the returns it is able to achieve.

Recommendations for Members

Selection of relevant factors in a report can be a judgment call so members should maintain records indicating the nature of the research, and be able to supply additional information if it is requested by the client or other users of the report.

Encourage the firm to establish a rigorous method of reviewing research work and results.

Standard V(C) Record Retention

Members and Candidates must develop and maintain appropriate records to support their investment analyses, recommendations, actions, and other investment-related communications with clients and prospective clients.

Members must maintain research records that support the reasons for the analyst's conclusions and any investment actions taken. Such records are the property of the firm. All communications with clients through any medium, including emails and text messages, are records that must be retained.

A member who changes firms must re-create the analysis documentation supporting her recommendation using publicly available information or information obtained from the company and must not rely on memory or materials created at her previous firm.

Recommendations for Members

Maintain notes and documents to support all investment communications.

Recommendations for Firms

If no regulatory standards or firm policies are in place, the Standard recommends a seven-year minimum holding period.

STANDARD VI: CONFLICTS OF INTEREST

Standard VI(A) Disclosure of Conflicts

Members and Candidates must make full and fair disclosure of all matters that could reasonably be expected to impair their independence and objectivity or interfere with respective duties to their clients, prospective clients, and employer. Members and Candidates must ensure that such disclosures are prominent, are delivered in plain language, and communicate the relevant information effectively.

Members must fully disclose to clients, prospects, and their employers all actual and potential conflicts of interest in order to protect investors and employers. These disclosures must be clearly stated.

The requirement that all potential areas of conflict be disclosed allows clients and prospects to judge motives and potential biases for themselves. Disclosure of broker-dealer market-making activities would be included here. Board service is another area of potential conflict.

The most common conflict that requires disclosure is actual ownership of stock in companies that the member recommends or that clients hold.

Another common source of conflicts of interest is a member's compensation/bonus structure, which can potentially create incentives to take actions that produce immediate gains for the member with little or no concern for longer-term returns for the client. Such conflicts must be disclosed when the member is acting in an advisory capacity and must be updated in the case of significant change in compensation structure.

Members must give their employers enough information to judge the impact of a conflict, take reasonable steps to avoid conflicts, and report them promptly if they occur.

Recommendations for Members

Any special compensation arrangements, bonus programs, commissions, performance-based fees, options on the firm's stock, and other incentives should be disclosed to clients. If the firm refuses to allow this disclosure, document the refusal and consider disassociating from the firm.

Standard VI(B) Priority of Transactions

Investment transactions for clients and employers must have priority over investment transactions in which a Member or Candidate is the beneficial owner.

Client transactions take priority over personal transactions and over transactions made on behalf of the member's firm. Personal transactions include situations where the member is a beneficial owner.

Personal transactions may be undertaken only after clients and the member's employer have had an adequate opportunity to act on a recommendation. Note that family member accounts that are client accounts should be treated just like any client account; they should not be disadvantaged.

Members must not act on information about pending trades for personal gain. The overriding considerations with respect to personal trades are that they do not disadvantage any clients.

When requested, members must fully disclose to investors their firm's personal trading policies.

Recommendations for Members

Members should encourage their firms to adopt the procedures listed in the following recommendations for firms and disclose these to clients.

Recommendations for Firms

All firms should have basic procedures in place that address conflicts created by personal investing. The following areas should be included:

- Establish limitations on employee participation in equity IPOs and systematically review such participation.
- Establish restrictions on participation in private placements. Strict limits should be placed on employee acquisition of these securities and proper supervisory procedures should be in place. Participation in these investments raises conflict of interest issues similar to those of IPOs.
- Establish blackout/restricted periods. Employees involved in investment decision making should have blackout periods prior to trading for clients—no front running (i.e., purchase or sale of securities in advance of anticipated client or employer purchases and sales). The size of the firm and the type of security should help dictate how severe the blackout requirement should be.
- Establish reporting procedures, including duplicate trade confirmations, disclosure of personal holdings and beneficial ownership positions, and preclearance procedures.
- Disclose, upon request, the firm's policies regarding personal trading.

Standard VI(C) Referral Fees

Members and Candidates must disclose to their employer, clients, and prospective clients, as appropriate, any compensation, consideration, or benefit received from or paid to others for the recommendation of products or services.

Members must inform employers, clients, and prospects of any benefit received for referrals of customers and clients, allowing them to evaluate the full cost of the service as well as any potential partiality. All types of consideration must be disclosed.

Recommendations for Members

Members should encourage their firms to adopt clear procedures regarding compensation for referrals.

Recommendations for Firms

Have an investment professional advise the clients at least quarterly on the nature and amount of any such compensation.

STANDARD VII: RESPONSIBILITIES AS A CFA INSTITUTE MEMBER OR CFA CANDIDATE

Standard VII(A) Conduct as Participants in CFA Institute Programs

Members and Candidates must not engage in any conduct that compromises the reputation or integrity of CFA Institute or the CFA designation or the integrity, validity, or security of CFA Institute programs.

Members must not engage in any activity that undermines the integrity of the CFA charter. This Standard applies to conduct that includes:

- Cheating on the CFA exam or any exam.
- Revealing anything about either broad or specific topics tested, content of exam questions, or formulas required or not required on the exam.
- Not following rules and policies of the CFA Program.
- Giving confidential information on the CFA Program to candidates or the public.
- Improperly using the designation to further personal and professional goals.
- Misrepresenting information on the Professional Conduct Statement (PCS) or the CFA Institute Professional Development Program.

Members and candidates are not precluded from expressing their opinions regarding the exam program or CFA Institute but must not reveal confidential information about the CFA Program.

Candidates who violate any of the CFA exam policies (e.g., calculator, personal belongings, Candidate Pledge) have violated Standard VII(A).

Members who volunteer in the CFA Program may not solicit or reveal information about questions considered for or included on a CFA exam, about the grading process, or about scoring of questions.

Standard VII(B) Reference to CFA Institute, the CFA Designation, and the CFA Program

When referring to CFA Institute, CFA Institute membership, the CFA designation, or candidacy in the CFA Program, Members and Candidates must not misrepresent or exaggerate the meaning or implications of membership in CFA Institute, holding the CFA designation, or candidacy in the CFA Program.

Members must not make promotional promises or guarantees tied to the CFA designation, such as over-promising individual competence or over-promising investment results in the future (i.e., higher performance, less risk, etc.).

Members must satisfy these requirements to maintain membership:

- Sign the PCS annually.
- Pay CFA Institute membership dues annually.

If they fail to do this, they are no longer active members.

Do not misrepresent or exaggerate the meaning of the CFA designation.

There is no partial CFA designation. It is acceptable to state that a candidate successfully completed the program in three years if, in fact, he did, but claiming superior ability because of this is not permitted.

The Chartered Financial Analyst and CFA marks must always be used either after a charterholder's name or as adjectives, but not as nouns, in written and oral communications.

The CFA designation should not be used in pseudonyms, such as online profile names, because CFA Institute must be able to verify that an individual has earned the right to use the CFA designation.

Recommendations for Members

Members should be sure that their firms are aware of the proper references to a member's CFA designation or candidacy, as errors in these references are common.

CONCEPT CHECKERS

1. In situations where the laws of a member or candidate's country of residence, the local laws of regions where the member or candidate does business, and the Code and Standards specify different requirements, the member or candidate must abide by:
   A. local law or the Code and Standards, whichever is stricter.
   B. the Code and Standards or his country's laws, whichever are stricter.
   C. the strictest of local law, his country's laws, or the Code and Standards.

2. According to the Standard on independence and objectivity, members and candidates:
   A. may accept gifts or bonuses from clients.
   B. may not accept compensation from an issuer of securities in return for producing research on those securities.
   C. should consider credit ratings issued by recognized agencies to be objective measures of credit quality.

3. Bill Cooper finds a table of historical bond yields on the website of the U.S. Treasury that supports the work he has done in his analysis and includes the table as part of his report without citing the source. Has Cooper violated the Code and Standards?
   A. Yes, because he did not cite the source of the table.
   B. Yes, because he did not verify the accuracy of the information.
   C. No, because the table is from a recognized source of financial or statistical data.

4. Which of the following statements about the Standard on misconduct is *most accurate*?
   A. Misconduct applies only to a member or candidate's professional activities.
   B. Neglecting to perform due diligence when required is an example of misconduct.
   C. A member or candidate commits misconduct by engaging in any illegal activity, such as a parking ticket offense.

5. Ed Ingus, CFA, visits the headquarters and main plant of Bullitt Company and observes that inventories of unsold goods appear unusually large. From the CFO, he learns that a recent increase in returned items may result in earnings for the current quarter that are below analysts' estimates. Bullitt plans to make this conclusion public next week. Based on his visit, Ingus changes his recommendation on Bullitt to "Sell." Has Ingus violated the Standard concerning material nonpublic information?
   A. Yes.
   B. No, because the information he used is not material.
   C. No, because his actions are consistent with the mosaic theory.

6.   Green Brothers, an emerging market fund manager, has two of its subsidiaries simultaneously buy and sell emerging market stocks. In its marketing literature, Green Brothers cites the overall emerging market volume as evidence of the market's liquidity. As a result of its actions, more investors participate in the emerging markets fund. Green Brothers *most likely*:
     A.   did not violate the Code and Standards.
     B.   violated the Standard regarding market manipulation.
     C.   violated the Standard regarding performance presentation.

7.   Cobb, Inc., has hired Jude Kasten, CFA, to manage its pension fund. The client(s) to whom Kasten owes her primary duty of loyalty is:
     A.   Cobb's management.
     B.   the shareholders of Cobb, Inc.
     C.   the beneficiaries of the pension fund.

8.   Which of the following actions is *most likely* a violation of the Standard on fair dealing?
     A.   A portfolio manager allocates IPO shares to all client accounts where it is suitable, including her brother's fee-based retirement account.
     B.   An investment firm routinely begins trading for its own account immediately after announcing recommendation changes to clients.
     C.   After releasing a general recommendation to all clients, an analyst calls the firm's largest institutional clients to discuss the recommendation in more detail.

9.   The Standard regarding suitability *most likely* requires that:
     A.   an advisor must analyze an investment's suitability for the client prior to recommending or acting on the investment.
     B.   a member or candidate must decline to carry out an unsolicited transaction that she believes is unsuitable for the client.
     C.   when managing an index fund, a manager who is evaluating potential investments must consider their suitability for the fund's shareholders.

10. Which of the following is *most likely* a recommended procedure for complying with the Standard on performance presentation?
     A.   Exclude terminated accounts from past performance history.
     B.   Present the performance of a representative account to show how a composite has performed.
     C.   Consider the level of financial knowledge of the audience to whom the performance is presented.

11. The CFA Institute Professional Conduct Program (PCP) has begun an investigation into Chris Jones, a Level II CFA candidate, and a number of his CFA Charterholder colleagues. Jones has access to confidential client records that could be useful in clearing his name and wishes to share this information with the PCP. Which of the following *most accurately* describes Jones's duties with regard to preservation of confidentiality?
    A. Sharing the confidential information with the PCP would violate the Standards.
    B. Jones may share confidential client information with the PCP.
    C. Jones may share confidential information about former clients with the PCP but may not share confidential information about current clients.

12. Connie Fletcher, CFA, works for a small money management firm that specializes in pension accounts. Recently, a friend asked her to act as an unpaid volunteer manager for the city's street sweep pension fund. As part of the position, the city would grant Fletcher a free parking space in front of her downtown office. Before Fletcher accepts, she should *most appropriately*:
    A. do nothing because this is a volunteer position.
    B. inform her current clients in writing and discuss the offer with her employer.
    C. disclose the details of the volunteer position to her employer and obtain written permission from her employer.

13. Sarah Johnson, a portfolio manager, is offered a bonus directly by a client if Johnson meets certain performance goals. To comply with the Standard that governs additional compensation arrangements, Johnson should:
    A. decline to accept a bonus outside of her compensation from her employer.
    B. disclose this arrangement to her employer in writing and obtain her employer's permission.
    C. disclose this arrangement to her employer only if she actually meets the performance goals and receives the bonus.

14. A member or candidate who has supervisory responsibility:
    A. should place particular emphasis on enforcing investment-related compliance policies.
    B. is responsible for providing adequate instruction and supervision over those to whom he has delegated authority.
    C. has complied with the Standards if she reports employee violations to upper management and provides a written warning to the employee to cease such activities.

15. Which of the following actions is a *required*, rather than *recommended*, action under the Standard regarding diligence and a reasonable basis for a firm's research recommendations?
    A. Compensate analysts based on a measure of the quality of their research.
    B. Review the assumptions used and evaluate the objectivity of third-party research reports.
    C. Have a policy requiring that research reports and recommendations have a basis that can be substantiated as reasonable and adequate.

16. Claire Marlin, CFA, manages an investment fund specializing in foreign currency trading. Marlin writes a report to investors based on an expected appreciation of the euro relative to other major currencies. Marlin shows the projected returns from the strategy under three favorable scenarios: if the euro appreciates less than 5%, between 5% and 10%, or more than 10%. She clearly states that these forecasts are her opinion. Has Marlin violated the Standard related to communication with clients?
    A. Yes.
    B. No, because she disclosed the basic characteristics of the investment.
    C. No, because she distinguished fact from opinion and discussed how the strategy may perform under a range of scenarios.

17. If regulations do not specify how long to retain the documents that support an analyst's conclusions, the Code and Standards recommend a period of at least:
    A. five years.
    B. seven years.
    C. ten years.

18. Daniel Lyons, CFA, is an analyst who covers several stocks including Horizon Company. Lyons's aunt owns 30,000 shares of Horizon. She informs Lyons that she has created a trust in his name into which she has placed 2,000 shares of Horizon. The trust is structured so that Lyons will not be able to sell the shares until his aunt dies, but may vote the shares. Lyons is due to update his research coverage of Horizon next week. Lyons should *most appropriately*:
    A. update the report as usual because he is not a beneficial owner of the stock.
    B. advise his superiors that he is no longer able to issue research recommendations on Horizon.
    C. disclose the situation to his employer and, if then asked to prepare a report, also disclose his beneficial ownership of the shares in his report.

19. Kate Wilson, CFA, is an equity analyst. Wilson enters two transactions for her personal account. Wilson sells 500 shares of Tibon, Inc., a stock on which she currently has a "Buy" recommendation. Wilson buys 200 shares of Hayfield Co. and the following day issues a research report on Hayfield with a "Buy" recommendation. Has Wilson violated the Code and Standards?
    A. No.
    B. Yes, both of her actions violate the Code and Standards.
    C. Yes, but only one of her actions violates the Code and Standards.

20. Hern Investments provides monthly emerging market research to Baker Brokerage in exchange for prospective client referrals and European equity research from Baker. Clients and prospects of Hern are not made aware of the agreement, but clients unanimously rave about the high quality of the research provided by Baker. As a result of the research, many clients with non-discretionary accounts have earned substantial returns on their portfolios. Managers at Hern have also used the research to earn outstanding returns for the firm's discretionary accounts. Hern has *most likely*:
    A. not violated the Code and Standards.
    B. violated the Code and Standards by using third-party research in discretionary accounts.
    C. violated the Code and Standards by failing to disclose the referral agreement with Baker.

21.   After writing the CFA Level III exam, Cynthia White goes to internet discussion site *CFA Haven* to express her frustration. White writes, "CFA Institute is not doing a competent job of evaluating candidates because none of the questions in the June exam touched on Alternative Investments." White *most likely* violated the Standard related to conduct as a candidate in the CFA program by:
   A.   publicly disputing CFA Institute policies and procedures.
   B.   disclosing subject matter covered or not covered on a CFA exam.
   C.   participating in an internet forum that is directed toward CFA Program participants.

22.   After passing all three levels of the CFA exams on her first attempts and being awarded her CFA Charter, Paula Osgood is promoting her new money management firm by issuing an advertisement. Which of these statements would *most likely* violate the Standard related to use of the CFA designation?
   A.   "To earn the right to use the CFA designation, Paula passed three exams covering ethics, financial statement analysis, asset valuation, and portfolio management."
   B.   "Paula passed three 6-hour exams on her first attempts and is a member of her local investment analyst society."
   C.   "Because of her extensive training, Paula will be able to achieve better investment results than managers who have not been awarded the CFA designation."

ANSWERS – CONCEPT CHECKERS

1. **C**   To comply with Standard I(A) Knowledge of the Law, a member must always abide by the strictest applicable law, regulation, or standard.

2. **A**   Gifts from clients are acceptable under Standard I(B) Independence and Objectivity, but the Standard requires members and candidates to disclose such gifts to their employers. Standard I(B) allows issuer-paid research as long as the analysis is thorough, independent, unbiased, and has a reasonable and adequate basis for its conclusions, and the compensation from the issuer is disclosed. Members and candidates should consider the potential for conflicts of interest inherent in credit ratings and may need to do independent research to evaluate the soundness of these ratings.

3. **C**   According to Standard I(C) Misrepresentation, members and candidates must cite the sources of the information they use in their analysis, unless the information is factual data (as opposed to analysis or opinion) from a recognized financial or statistical reporting service. The U.S. Treasury is one example of a recognized source of factual data.

4. **B**   Failing to act when required by one's professional obligations, such as neglecting to perform due diligence related to an investment recommendation, violates Standard I(D) Misconduct. Acts a member commits outside his professional capacity are misconduct if they reflect poorly on the member or candidate's honesty, integrity, or competence (e.g., theft or fraud). Violations of the law that do not reflect on the member or candidate's honesty, integrity, or competence (e.g., an act related to civil disobedience or minor civil offenses) are not necessarily regarded as misconduct.

5. **A**   The statement from the CFO about the current quarter's earnings is material nonpublic information. Ingus violated Standard II(A) Material Nonpublic Information by acting or causing others to act on it.

6. **B**   The intent of Green Brothers' actions is to manipulate the appearance of market liquidity in order to attract investment to its own funds. The increased trading activity was not based on market fundamentals or an actual trading strategy to benefit investors. It was merely an attempt to mislead market participants in order to increase assets under Green Brothers' management. The action violates Standard II(B) Market Manipulation.

7. **C**   She has a responsibility to all three but her first obligation is to the clients. In many countries, that is especially true for defined benefit plans.

8. **B**   The firm must give its clients an opportunity to act on recommendation changes. Firms can offer different levels of service to clients as long as this is disclosed to all clients. The largest institutional clients would likely be paying higher fees for a greater level of service. The portfolio manager's brother's account should be treated the same as any other client account.

9. **A**   According to Standard III(C) Suitability, a member or candidate who is in an advisory relationship with a client is responsible for analyzing the suitability of an investment for the client before taking investment action or making a recommendation. If a member or candidate believes an unsolicited trade is unsuitable for a client, the appropriate action is to discuss the trade with the client. The advisor may follow her firm's policies for obtaining client approval if the requested trade would not affect the risk and return of the client's portfolio materially. If the trade would have a material effect, the advisor should discuss with the client whether the IPS needs to be updated. When managing a fund to an index or stated mandate, the manager is responsible for ensuring that potential investments are consistent with the fund's mandate. Suitability for individuals would be a concern for an advisor who recommends the fund to clients, but not for the manager of the fund.

10. **C**   Recommendations stated in Standard III(D) Performance Presentation include considering the sophistication and knowledge of the audience when presenting performance data. Other recommendations are to include terminated accounts in past performance history; to present the performance of a composite as a weighted average of the performance of similar portfolios, rather than using a single representative account; and to maintain the records and data that were used to calculate performance.

11. **B**   Members and candidates are required to cooperate with PCP investigations into their own conduct and encouraged to cooperate with PCP investigations into the conduct of others. Sharing confidential information with the PCP is not a violation of Standard III(E) Preservation of Confidentiality. Any client information shared with the PCP will be kept in strict confidence. There is no distinction between sharing confidential information of current versus former clients.

12. **C**   According to Standard IV(A) Loyalty, members and candidates are expected to act for the benefit of their employer and not deprive the employer of their skills. Fletcher is performing work similar to the services that her employer provides. Whether it is voluntary is not material to the need to disclose the details of the position to her employer and get written permission before accepting the position. Informing her other clients (i.e., the clients of her employer) is not normally appropriate; the issue is with her employer.

13. **B**   Johnson should disclose her additional compensation arrangement in writing to her employer and obtain her employer's written consent before accepting this offer, in accordance with Standard IV(B) Additional Compensation Arrangements.

14. **B**   Members or candidates may delegate supervisory duties to subordinates but remain responsible for instructing and supervising them. Reporting the violation and warning the employee are not sufficient to comply with Standard IV(C) Responsibilities of Supervisors. The supervisor must also take steps to prevent further violations while she conducts an investigation, such as limiting the employee's activity or increasing her monitoring of the employee. Supervisors should enforce investment-related and non-investment related policies equally.

15. **B**   Standard V(A) Diligence and Reasonable Basis requires analysts who use third-party research to review its assumptions and evaluate the independence and objectivity of the research. The other choices are recommended procedures for compliance with the Standard.

16. **A** Standard V(B) Communication with Clients and Prospective Clients requires that members and candidates communicate the risk associated with the investment strategy used and how the strategy is expected to perform in a range of scenarios. Marlin should have also discussed how her strategy would perform if the euro depreciates instead of appreciating as she expects.

17. **B** When no other regulatory guidance applies, Standard V(C) Record Retention recommends that records be maintained for a minimum of seven years.

18. **C** Even though the shares are held in trust, Lyons is considered a beneficial owner under Standard VI(A) Disclosure of Conflicts because he has a pecuniary interest in the shares and because has the power to vote the shares. Lyons is obligated to inform his employer of the potential conflict. If Lyons's employer permits him to continue issuing investment recommendations on the company, Lyons must disclose the existence of a potential conflict in his reports.

19. **B** Standard VI(B) Priority of Transactions requires members and candidates to give clients an adequate opportunity to act on a recommendation before trading for accounts in which the member or candidate has a beneficial ownership interest. Members and candidates may trade for their own accounts as long as they do not disadvantage clients, benefit personally from client trades, or violate any regulations that apply. Under Standard VI(A), she must avoid conflicts or appearances of conflicts of interest. At the very least, she should consult with her supervisor or compliance officer before selling a stock she is recommending.

20. **C** According to Standard VI(C) Referral Fees, Hern must disclose the referral arrangement between itself and Baker so that potential clients can judge the true cost of Hern's services and assess whether there is any partiality inherent in the recommendation of services.

21. **B** Standard VII(A) Conduct as Participants in CFA Institute Programs prohibits candidates from revealing which portions of the Candidate Body of Knowledge were or were not covered on an exam. Members and candidates are free to disagree with the policies, procedures, or positions taken by the CFA Institute. The Standard does not prohibit participating in CFA Program-related internet blogs, forums, or social networks.

22. **C** Standard VII(B) Reference to CFA Institute, the CFA Designation, and the CFA Program prohibits members and candidates from implying superior performance as a result of being a CFA charterholder. Concise factual descriptions of the requirements to obtain the CFA Charter are acceptable. Osgood's statement that she passed the exams on her first attempts is acceptable because it states a fact.

APPLICATION OF THE CODE AND STANDARDS

Study Session 2

EXAM FOCUS

The cases are not intended to teach new material, but to provide additional examples of application of the Standards.

 Professor's Note: This case addresses conflicts of interest and methods to avoid current or potential conflicts.

LOS 3.a: Evaluate professional conduct and formulate an appropriate response to actions that violate the Code of Ethics and Standards of Professional Conduct.

LOS 3.b: Formulate appropriate policy and procedural changes needed to assure compliance with the Code of Ethics and Standards of Professional Conduct.

CASE OUTLINE: THE CONSULTANT

Mark Vernley, CFA, is a petroleum engineer and owns an engineering consulting firm called Energetics, Inc. Energetics consults on asset and project valuations. Vernley has a large personal portfolio that includes a sizable investment in energy-related securities, including Highridge Oil Pipelines.

Energetics' employees are expected to be honest, fair, and to avoid potential conflicts of interest. Vernley is well-respected by his peers. However, Energetics does not have a formal compliance system in place.

Vernley was recently asked to write a proposal to help resolve conflicts between Highridge Oil Pipelines and several of Highridge's clients (oil shippers). Vernley's proposal was accepted by the appropriate regulatory agencies and was ready for implementation when Plains Pipeline Systems filed an objection with the regulatory agency claiming that Vernley's stock holdings constituted a conflict of interest. Although the regulatory agency discarded Plains Pipeline's objection, Vernley is concerned that his business could be hurt by further allegations of conflicts of interest.

Discussion: Conflicts of Interest in a Personal Portfolio

There are *two* approaches for dealing with potential conflicts of interest:

1. Avoidance through any of several methods:
   - *Refrain from investing in sensitive industries.*
   - *Establish a "blind trust."* In a blind trust, control of the portfolio is turned over to a manager who has full discretion over portfolio assets within the guidelines that have been established. The beneficiary does not know the composition of the portfolio except at certain reporting periods.
   - *Invest in mutual funds.* A mutual fund investment removes you from the direct investment decision-making process.

2. *Disclosure.* An alternative to avoidance is full disclosure of all potential conflicts of interest.

Discussion: Need for a Formal Compliance System

Energetics needs a formal compliance system established to avoid the potential for future conflicts of interest. Compliance programs have several key elements, including:

1. *Communication.* The employees must be informed of the standards and procedures which apply to them. The CFA Institute Code and Standards can serve as a basis for a more formal compliance system.

2. *Education.* Employees must be educated regarding the impact and implementation of the compliance system.

Compliance Procedures

Written compliance documents. The compliance program must be well documented for it to succeed. The following are ways to document compliance:

- Receive annual certification from employees that they are familiar with the standards and agree to conform to them.
- Require employees to report personal trades at least quarterly, including securities in which they hold a beneficial interest.
- Disclose to management any additional compensation from outside sources.
- Receive certification from employees that they are not competing with their employer. This also protects the firm.
- Receive information from employees of any certifications or standards required to continue in their profession.

Corporate Culture and Leadership

Corporate credos can be used to instill an ethical culture in the firm. The purpose of the credo is to infuse a set of guiding principles that members of the firm can follow so that the firm as a whole is an ethical entity. For a corporate credo to work, the firm's leadership must embrace its content. Corporate ethics work from the top down.

Professor's Note: Pearl Investment Management (A) centers on the responsibilities of supervisors and employees within a firm, trading in client securities for personal accounts, and divulging confidential client information.

CASE OUTLINE: CASE A

Peter Sherman recently attained an MBA in finance and took a position at Pearl Investment Management as an account manager. Pearl is an investment counseling firm that deals with portfolio and endowment management along with some large individual accounts. Research is maintained in house to reduce Pearl's reliance on brokerage firm research, to compare with prevailing opinions, and to analyze companies that are not followed in great depth.

Pearl's internal compliance policy should be consistent with the Code of Ethics and Standards of Professional Conduct because of the large number of CFA charterholders employed. Its policy manual also includes applicable laws and regulations that affect Pearl's operations and employee conduct. All employees are required to read and sign a statement declaring their knowledge of Pearl's policies, both when they join the firm and annually thereafter.

Sherman was required by his supervisor to read the policy manual and sign the compliance sheet as part of his orientation. His supervisor directed him to the compliance department if he had any questions. Sherman read the manual quickly and signed the compliance sheet. After a few months, Sherman is confident in his duties as an account manager. He is challenged by his duties and enjoys the close access to investment information and strategies. His own savings plan has benefited from his greater insight and comprehension.

Prior to his new position, Sherman invested his savings in no-load mutual funds. He is now looking for a greater return by creating his own portfolio. His interest in investing for his future has led him to read books on investments and portfolio strategy. Sherman enjoys talking about his newfound knowledge with friends and relatives. To begin the pursuit of his own portfolio, Sherman opened an account with a well-known discount broker and purchased a few of the stocks touted by Pearl.

Questions arising from this case include the following:

- What role is required of supervisors in the firm's compliance with its policies?

  Supervisors must take an active role in the firm's compliance with its policies. Employees must be fully aware of the firm's policies and should consult their supervisor or compliance department if they have any questions or uncertainty.

- What priority do client trades take over personal trades?

  Personal trades cannot be executed before or during client transactions. Investment professionals must make sure that their holdings do not compromise their ethical standards.

- What duty exists regarding a firm's use of proprietary information?

  Care must be taken not to divulge proprietary information to non-clients.

DISCUSSION

The possible violations relate to supervisory responsibilities, the obligation to follow all applicable laws and regulations, the standards for trading in personal accounts, and the ban against transmitting confidential information.

Knowledge of the Law—Governing Laws and Regulations

Sherman has the responsibility of knowing all governing laws, and his supervisor also has a responsibility to educate and train employees. Sherman's brief introduction to the firm's policies and procedures and being told to go to the compliance office if he has questions do not constitute sufficient education and training. He should be informed of the firm's compliance with the CFA Institute Code and Standards. Although not technically bound by the Code and Standards himself, Sherman is obliged to abide by Pearl's policies and procedures.

Knowledge of the Law—Legal and Ethical Violations

Remember that supervisors, managers, and employees cannot *knowingly* participate in a violation of the Code and Standards. In order to properly recognize violations, they must be made aware of all facts giving rise to the violations.

> **Actions required:** Sherman's supervisor needs to more actively monitor Sherman's and all employees' activities.

Responsibilities of Supervisors

Remember that according to Standard IV(C) Responsibilities of Supervisors, supervisors must make reasonable attempts to find out about and prevent violations of applicable laws or regulations and the Code and Standards. Just the existence of a compliance manual does not release the supervisor from responsibility. Education of employees must be ongoing.

Trading in Client Securities for Personal Accounts

Sherman may be in violation of Standard III(B) Fair Dealing and Standard VI(B) Priority of Transactions if he is trading in securities which are being actively pursued for Pearl's client accounts. His prior position in a mutual fund was not in violation because he did not have an inside track to the fund's management and relevant information.

Members of Pearl cannot trade in their own accounts before or during transactions that are instigated for the benefit of clients. This restriction includes both personal accounts and any other account in which they have a beneficial interest. Client portfolios always take precedence over personal trades. Sherman's actions may constitute *front-running* if he is trading before clients.

> **Actions required:** Before placing personal orders, Sherman should get them approved by Compliance. He should never take actions ahead of clients.

Conveying Confidential Client Information

Sherman has a duty to uphold the propriety of Pearl's investment strategy. Divulging confidential information through his own investment activities or in discussions with friends and family is a breach under Standard IV(A) Loyalty and Standard III(A) Loyalty, Prudence, and Care. Sherman has breached a special trust.

Actions required: Sherman must not share specific investment recommendations or information about client accounts. This would be a fiduciary breach to the firm and its clients. If unsure, Sherman should consult with Compliance.

Professor's Note: Pearl Investment Management (B) involves issues related to a candidate's compliance responsibilities, equitable treatment of clients, the fiduciary duties owed to clients, the appropriateness of investment recommendations, and the process of correcting trading errors in client accounts.

CASE OUTLINE: CASE B

Peter Sherman, now a CFA candidate, has recently been assigned a special project related to problems in the misallocation of block trades among larger clients of Pearl. He was given the assignment based on his accounting experience and because none of his clients were involved (even though the majority of his accounts are *total rate of return* portfolios). The most complicated misallocation involved the initial public offering (IPO) of Gene Alteration Research Corporation. As team leader, Sherman corrected the portfolios that had transactions associated with the block trades. Part of the reconciliation involved shifting particular securities among accounts. After his adjustments, Sherman feels that all the transactions have been corrected and all clients have been treated fairly. He still wonders how the problems arose.

Because his review was hurried, Sherman did not have time to look over the individual clients' investment policy statements. He is certain that portfolio managers would direct only appropriate trades to the accounts of their clients. He is assured by the fact that the trading desk acts as a second check for the investment guidelines of clients. Gene Alteration Research Corporation has a conservative investment policy.

Issues raised in this case include the following:

- Did Sherman comply with the Code and Standards?

    Sherman relied on others' knowledge of the Code and Standards rather than his own.

- Have fiduciary duties been breached?

    None of Sherman's clients were included in the allocation of the IPO.

- Were the actions of the investment managers and the trading desk suitable for the clients based on their investment policy statements?

    An investment manager must determine in advance which accounts are appropriate for the new purchase by analyzing each account's objectives and constraints.

- Were corrections for trading errors in client accounts handled fairly?

  Client portfolios must be corrected in an appropriate manner and the reversal procedure handled fairly so that client portfolios do not bear unnecessary risk.

Discussion

Responsibility of Candidates to Comply with the Code and Standards

- As a CFA candidate, Sherman must depend more on his own knowledge of the Code of Ethics and the Standards of Professional Conduct with support from Pearl's compliance department. He cannot continue to rely on the company's explanation of the Standards.
- He is now susceptible to disciplinary action by CFA Institute. Because Pearl has incorporated many of the CFA Institute standards, much of his duty as a candidate to inform his employer of his higher obligation is relieved.

  Actions required: Sherman must once again familiarize himself with Pearl's personnel policy and CFA Institute's *Standards of Practice Handbook* so he can better understand the subtleties of the Standards.

Dealing with Clients—Responsibilities to Clients

Fiduciary duty to clients has not been protected, and all clients must be treated fairly. There has been a violation of Standard III(A) Loyalty, Prudence, and Care, which requires members to act in clients' best interest. When reallocating IPO trades, Sherman needs to make sure they are done in the clients' best interest and are suitable to the client.

Dealing with Clients—Fair Dealing

When reallocating block trades, members must ensure that Standard III(B) Fair Dealing is followed. Do not favor large accounts. In IPO distributions, Pearl must use some type of fair pro rata system.

  Actions required: Sherman must check and make sure that no client orders were entered that violated client guidelines. He must make sure that the allocation of block trades is done equitably.

Bearing the Financial Risk of Errors in Client Accounts

Client portfolios must not bear the risk of improper trades, and the firm must avoid shifting the burden to other accounts. The firm must take responsibility either directly or indirectly for improper transactions. Pearl should credit short-term interest to those accounts from which funds were removed to cover the trades.

Actions required: No client should have any financial loss. The firm should take the loss. Short-term interest should be credited to affected accounts.

Professor's Note: Pearl Investment Management (C) incorporates issues related to the appropriateness of investment recommendations, the use of insider information, failure to conform to the highest ethical standards, and neglecting to obey governing laws and standards.

CASE OUTLINE: CASE C

After Peter Sherman passes Level II of the CFA® program, Tomas Champa, the head of Pearl's research division, has Sherman transferred to the research department. Sherman graciously accepts the transfer with the understanding that he could possibly be promoted from his junior analyst position when he passes Level III of the CFA program.

Champa remained in the United States after a 5-year stint working for a major international bank. He is not a CFA charterholder, but he has a great deal of practical experience. Champa is very excited about leading Pearl's new research work in international securities. He wishes to start with companies in developing countries whose economies have boomed in recent years. He tells his analysts to come up with emerging market research recommendations quickly or be scrutinized by management and clients.

Although Sherman is new to the department, Champa assigns him the difficult tasks because of his lack of biased notions about emerging market companies. Sherman is to center his efforts on Latin and South America, areas in which Champa believes he has special insights and can direct Sherman.

Sherman reads several brokerage reports on Latin American markets and has a discussion with Champa and the other analysts about trends in Latin and South America in relation to the historical environment in the United States. He also scans the statistical section of S&P's *International Stock Guide.*

Champa refers Sherman to Gonzalo Alves, who is well connected in Mexico and on the board of directors of several large Mexican firms. Alves tells Sherman about the Mexican economy and the companies he oversees as a director. He tells about the strategic direction of each company, some potential targets, and how variances in the Mexican economy will affect each company. Sherman believes the information Alves has given him will be quite useful in writing his reports, and he feels comfortable in doing so.

Sherman is assigned the project of generating a research report on several Mexican telecommunication and cable companies. Champa gives Sherman a deadline that does not allow him to do in-depth analysis and research. He finishes his report hastily by relying on excerpts from brokerage reports, trends, and ratios from the S&P *International Stock Guide* and on the opinions of Alves. He concludes with an internal *buy* recommendation for larger Pearl clients. Sherman does not cite the brokerage reports because they are widely read and distributed in the investment community.

Champa and his staff get a great deal of recognition for their timely response to market demand, and the portfolio managers ask them for additional recommendations. Champa brings together his staff the next day to assign additional Latin American industries to be researched. At the meeting, Jill Grant, who is also a CFA candidate, questions Sherman as to the lack of detail on the Mexican economy or historical exchange rate volatility between the peso and the U.S. dollar. She is concerned with the comparability of Mexican and American securities. Grant stresses that diversification occurs only when global markets have little correlation with the U.S. market. Sherman responds by stating, "Our clients are sophisticated investors; they know these things already." Champa supports his opinion. Several issues emerge from this case.

- Did Sherman exercise proper care and independent judgment in rendering his opinions?

  The case points out that Sherman's work was rushed due to pressure placed on Sherman from Champa.

- Did Sherman's conversation with Alves result in the use of material nonpublic information in his research recommendations?

  Alves shared information with Sherman on companies he oversees as a director. This information included the strategic direction, potential targets, and economic vulnerabilities that existed within each company.

- Did Sherman violate the Standards with respect to acknowledging the research of others used in his report?

  Only generally recognized public sources can be used without reference.

- Did Sherman have a *reasonable basis for his research opinion?*

  Sherman effectively used the recommendations of others, which may have had a reasonable basis or not.

- Can Sherman's research be considered "independent"? Is Sherman using reasonable judgment by accepting Champa's conjecture on the direction of the Mexican economy?

  Sherman should cite the brokerage reports to help provide a basis for his conclusions as well as recognize the input of others.

Discussion

Proper Care and Independent Judgment

By giving in to Champa's pressure to expedite his research, Sherman is violating Standard V(A) Diligence and Reasonable Basis. He did not use suitable care or render independent professional judgment.

Actions required: Sherman must remind Champa of the responsibility to follow the necessary steps in performing research and in the portfolio decision-making process. The analysis must not be rushed.

Use of Insider Information

- Sherman has potentially violated Standard II(A) Material Nonpublic Information.
- Sherman's discussion about the Mexican market and several significant corporations with Alves may be illegal if material nonpublic information was transmitted.
- Champa and Alves may not be aware of the ethical violation committed because they are most familiar with foreign laws and customs. CFA charterholders are prohibited from using confidential information for their personal use or that of their clients. Local laws and customs are irrelevant because it is a violation of U.S. law and the CFA Institute Code of Ethics and the Standards of Professional Conduct.
- The case does not mention the *mosaic theory* which adds a clearer picture of the role of an analyst. The theory states that an analyst can compile nonmaterial and/or public information to provide a useful insight into the direction of a corporation.
- One of the most difficult challenges to CFA charterholders is reconciling CFA Institute Code and Standards with foreign laws, customs, and regulations. Adhering to a higher standard is often to the disadvantage of CFA charterholders and many times to their clients.
- Honoring the interests of clients and the integrity of the investment profession is a top priority of CFA charterholders. Alves may have valuable information, but Sherman may use it only if it is both ethical and legal.

> **Actions required:** If Sherman has received material nonpublic information, he must disclose the fact to Pearl's compliance department. He must not use the information in his report in any fashion unless he makes a valid attempt to make it public knowledge. This process must be incorporated into the firm's policy statement.

Using the Research of Others

Acknowledgment of the use of others' research is required. Sherman must give credit to the research of others unless it is statistical in form and widely known to be public knowledge. Only recognized sources can be used without reference. His reliance on brokerage reports in his own work requires him to cite the author(s) or he is in violation of Standard I(C) Misrepresentation for committing plagiarism.

> **Actions required:** Sherman must give proper credit to the author(s) of any brokerage report he used in preparation of his own report.

Reasonable Basis for a Research Opinion

Sherman must be thorough in his recommendation, have a reasonable foundation, and avoid any misrepresentations. He basically took over the work and recommendations of other analysts. Whether or not the recommendations have a solid basis or present any misrepresentations is unknown. By not carrying out independent research, Sherman may have violated Standard V(A) Diligence and Reasonable Basis.

The time pressure placed on Sherman did not allow for a complete review of the industry in the context of the national and global economies, nor an analysis of specific companies in relation to each other. His use of a few brokerage reports cannot be considered "appropriate research and investigation."

Relevant Factors and Fact vs. Opinion in Research Reports

Sherman must use appropriate discretion in determining what to include in his report. If he does not do so, he has ignored his obligation to the firm's clients and violated Standard V(B) Communication with Clients and Prospective Clients. By accepting Alves's conjecture on the direction of the Mexican economy, Sherman is not using reasonable judgment.

Grant, the other junior researcher, is obligated as a CFA candidate to confront Sherman and Champa through the compliance department, if she is not satisfied with the rationale provided for not including the relevant information.

> **Actions required:** Sherman's report must be as complete as possible, supply a reasonable foundation for decisions, not misrepresent investment characteristics, and take into account the appropriateness of the investment for clients. All relevant factors must be considered in the investment recommendation.

Misrepresentation of Services and Performance Presentation

Depending on how Pearl informs its clients of their endeavor into the international sector, Pearl may be in violation of Standard I(C) Misrepresentation.

If Pearl cites a reaction to an evolving marketplace and the increased globalization of securities markets, no violation is evident. If Pearl is promoting its expertise in the international arena to gain new and existing clients, however, then a violation is quite evident.

Because Pearl is new to emerging markets, it cannot report actual performance on its investments until it has some meaningful concentration in the area or manages accounts made up entirely of emerging market securities. At this point, Pearl must make strong disclaimers as to the size of its emerging markets accounts and the timing of additions to the aggregate account.

> **Actions required:** Pearl cannot boast of any *track record* in emerging markets investments. However, Pearl can tell clients of its qualifications and the returns it may produce in comparison with a different environment in which it used similar methodology. This must be incorporated in Pearl's policy statement.

KEY CONCEPTS

LOS 3.a,b

The Consultant
- Conflicts, or perceived conflicts, must be disclosed in clear and plain language.

The firm should inform and educate employees regarding their ethical responsibilities.

Recommended procedures are:

- Annual certification of employees and quarterly reporting by employees.
- Disclose actual or potential sources of other compensation to employer.
- Certification by employees that they are not in competition with the employer.
- Employees are members of appropriate professional organizations.

Pearl Investment Management (A)
- A policy manual without training is inadequate.
- Do not share client information with family and friends.
- Do not trade ahead of clients, front running.
- Know applicable laws and regulations.
- Supervisors must actually supervise employee's activities.

Pearl Investment Management (B)
- When necessary, check the client IPS. Don't just assume.
- A CFA candidate is subject to disciplinary actions.
- Mistakes by the firm that penalize clients must be corrected without penalty to the client.
- Do not unfairly penalize smaller versus larger clients.

Pearl Investment Management (C)
- Supervisors should not exert inappropriate pressure that leads to unprofessional work.
- Do not use or seek material nonpublic information. If obtained, generally best to advise your compliance officer.
- Do not use the work of others without attribution (e.g., work from another's report).
- Don't misrepresent your level of expertise.
- Include all relevant information in a report, relevance requires good judgment.

ASSET MANAGER CODE OF PROFESSIONAL CONDUCT

EXAM FOCUS

The Asset Manager Code is specific to Level III. It applies to investment firms, not individuals. It largely duplicates and, in some cases, extends portfolio management-related requirements of the Standards of Professional Conduct.

THE ASSET MANAGER CODE

LOS 4.a: Explain the purpose of the Asset Manager Code and the benefits that may accrue to a firm that adopts the Code.

The Asset Manager Code (AMC) is global, voluntary, and applies to investment management firms. Firms are encouraged to adopt the AMC as a template and guidepost to ethical business practice in asset management. Adoption demonstrates that the firm is placing client interests first. The AMC is flexible and firms must develop their own policies and procedures, tailored to their business and clients, to ensure compliance with the AMC. The AMC provides guidance on risk management. Adoption benefits the firm as a step in gaining the trust and confidence of its clients.

LOS 4.b: Explain the ethical and professional responsibilities required by the six General Principles of Conduct of the Asset Manager Code.

LOS 4.c: Determine whether an asset manager's practices and procedures are consistent with the Asset Manager Code.

LOS 4.d: Recommend practices and procedures designed to prevent violations of the Asset Manager Code.

Professor's Note: These three LOS are inseparable. We will cover the six general principals of the AMC. Meeting the principals and requirements puts the firm in compliance. Unless an item in the following write up is denoted as recommended, it is a requirement.

Under each principal, we will also list the recommended practices and procedures (P&P). The recommendations are not requirements, but provide guidance on the type of policies and procedures the firm could use to meet the requirements and then claim compliance with the AMC. Adopting the recommended P&P (if relevant) will assist the firm in preventing violations of the AMC. The firm is still responsible for determining the specific P&P needed for their business. Not all sections of the AMC have recommendations.

There are many references to issues such as the client IPS, best execution, firm-wide risk management, and soft dollars that are covered elsewhere in the curriculum, so do not bog down on those. This is your initial study and the material makes more sense after you go through all the study sessions. You cannot know how pieces fit together until you see the whole curriculum. The intent of the Level III material is to be highly interconnected.

Once you read the material and/or watch our related videos, you should immediately work our questions and the end of chapter questions in the CFA reading for the AMC.

There are six components to the Asset Manager Code of Professional Conduct[1]:

A) Loyalty to Clients.
B) Investment Process and Actions.
C) Trading.
D) Risk Management, Compliance, and Support.
E) Performance and Valuation.
F) Disclosures.

Related to these components are six general principles of conduct:

- Always act ethically and professionally.
- Act in the best interest of the client.
- Act in an objective and independent manner.
- Perform actions using skill, competence, and diligence.
- Communicate accurately with clients on a regular basis.
- Comply with legal and regulatory requirements regarding capital markets.

A) Loyalty to Clients

1. Place the client's interest ahead of the firm's.

   Recommendations: Align manager compensation to avoid conflict with client best interests, such as avoiding an incentive for excessive risk taking in order to increase manager compensation.

---

[1] Reading 4, CFA Program Curriculum, Volume 1, Level III (CFA Institute, 2017).

2. Maintain client confidentiality.

    Recommendations: Create a privacy policy to document how such information is gathered, stored, and used. Include an anti-money laundering policy (if needed) to prevent the firm's involvement in illegal activities.

3. Refuse business relationships and gifts that would compromise independence, objectivity, and loyalty to clients.

    Recommendations: Refuse gifts and entertainment of more than minimal value from service providers. Establish written P&P to define appropriate limits for gifts from both service providers and clients. Require employees to disclose such gifts. Prohibit cash gifts. Managers may maintain other (significant) business relationships with clients as long as potential conflicts are managed and disclosed.

B) Investment Process and Actions

1. Use reasonable care and judgment in managing client assets. Managers should act as other knowledgeable professionals would act to balance risk and return for the client.

2. Do not manipulate price and volume in an effort to mislead market participants as this damages the integrity of markets to the detriment of all investors. Actions such as establishing large positions to distort prices or spreading false rumors are violations.

3. Deal fairly with all clients when providing information, advice, and taking actions. Managers may offer higher levels of service to some clients for higher compensation if the service levels are disclosed and available to all clients willing to pay for them. Managers can engage in secondary investment opportunities (that are offered as a result of other business activities) if the opportunity is fairly allocated to all suitable clients.

4. Have a reasonable and adequate basis for recommendations. The due diligence required will vary based on the complexity and risks of the strategy. Third-party research can be used if there is a reasonable basis to support it. Managers must be knowledgeable of the securities they recommend. This is particularly true for complex strategies and such strategies must be explained in understandable ways to the client.

5. For portfolios **managed to a specific style or strategy**, managers do not have to evaluate the suitability to a given client. Managers must provide suitable disclosure so clients can determine if the portfolio is suitable for their needs. The portfolio must then be managed in the manner intended. Flexibility and deviations from that intent must be expressly agreed to by clients.

    Recommendations: Disclose permitted deviations from intent as they occur (or in normal reporting). If the strategy or style of the portfolio changes, allow clients to redeem the investment without undue penalty.

6. When **managing portfolios of a specific client**, understand the client's objectives and constraints in order to take suitable actions for that client.

   Recommendations: Establish and update a written IPS for that client at least annually and as circumstances warrant. The IPS will specify the roles and responsibilities of the manager, and those will vary by situation. A performance benchmark to evaluate portfolio performance should be specified. Ideally, each investment decision will be made in the context of the client's total situation (but recognizing the client decides what information to share with the manager).

C) Trading

1. Do not act or cause others to act on material nonpublic information that could affect the value of public securities. Such actions are frequently illegal and damage the integrity of markets. Managers must adopt compliance procedures to segregate information between those with reasons to have such information and the rest of the firm.

   Recommendations: Managers can use procedures such as firewalls between those with reasons to have such information and the rest of the firm. They should develop procedures to evaluate whether company-specific information is material and nonpublic. Information on pending trades or holdings may be material nonpublic information.

2. Give clients priority over the firm. Managers cannot execute ahead of clients or to the detriment of clients' interests. Managers may invest their own capital along with clients if clients do not suffer.

   Recommendations: Develop P&P to monitor and limit personal trading by employees, require prior approval of investment in private placements and IPOs, and provide the compliance officer with employee personal transaction and holdings information. Establish a watch list of companies in which employees may not personally trade without approval.

3. Use client commissions only to pay for investment-related products and services that directly benefit the client, not for the management of the firm.

   Recommendations: Some managers have eliminated soft dollars. If soft dollars are used, disclose this to clients and adopt industry best practices such as the CFA Institute Soft Dollar Standards.

4. Seek best execution for all client trades.

   Recommendations: If clients direct trading, advise the clients it may compromise the manager's ability to seek best execution and seek written acknowledgement of this from the client.

5. Establish policies for fair and equitable trade allocation. All clients for whom the trade is suitable should be given the opportunity to participate.

Recommendations: Group suitable accounts and trade as a block (all participate at the same price) and allocate partial trades pro rata. Specifically address how IPOs and private placements are handled.

D) Risk Management, Compliance, and Support

1. Develop detailed P&Ps to comply with the AMC and all legal/regulatory requirements.

2. Appoint a competent, knowledgeable, credible compliance officer with authority to implement the P&Ps.

   Recommendations: The officer is independent of the investment and operations personnel. The officer reviews all firm and employee transactions. Require all employees to acknowledge they understand and comply with the AMC.

3. Use an independent third party to verify that information provided to clients is accurate and complete. Verification may be based on audit or reviews of pooled funds and account statements and transaction reports from the custodian bank for individual accounts (i.e., not just on internal records of the firm.)

4. Maintain records to document investment actions.

   Recommendations: Retain compliance records and documentation of violations and corrective actions. Retain for at least seven years or as required by law and regulations.

5. Employ sufficient and qualified staff to meet all AMC requirements. Managers must have (pay for) the resources to deliver the services promised and to assure compliance with the P&Ps.

6. Establish a business continuity plan to deal with disasters or market disruptions. At minimum this should include:
   * Backup (preferably offsite) of account information.
   * Plans to monitor, analyze, and trade investments.
   * Communication plans with key vendors and suppliers.
   * Employee communication and coverage of key business functions when normal communications are out.
   * Client communication plans.

7. Establish a firm-wide risk management plan to measure and manage the risks taken. It must be objective and independent of the influence of the portfolio managers.

   Recommendations: Consider outsourcing this process if needed. It may include stress and scenario testing. Be prepared to describe the process to clients.

E) Performance and Valuation

 Professor's Note: See the GIPS reading.

1. Present performance data that is fair, accurate, relevant, timely, and complete. Do not misrepresent performance of accounts or the firm.

    Recommendations: Adopt GIPS.

2. Use fair market prices when available and fair valuation in other cases.

    Recommendations: Independent third parties should be responsible for valuation to avoid conflicts of interest as manager fees are normally based on account value.

F) Disclosures

1. Ongoing, timely communication with clients using appropriate methods.

2. Ensure truthful, accurate, complete, and understandable communication. Use plain language. Determine what to disclose and how.

3. Include any (all) material facts regarding the firm, personnel, investments, and the investment process.

4. Disclose:
    *   Any conflicts of interest such as those arising from relationships with brokers and other clients, fees, soft dollars, bundled fees, directed brokerage, manager or employee holdings in the same securities as clients, and any other material issues.
    *   Regulatory and disciplinary actions related to professional conduct by the firm or employees.
    *   Investment process information including strategy, risk factors, lock-up period, derivatives, and leverage.
    *   Management fees and client costs including the method of their determination. Provide gross- and net-of-fee returns. Disclose any unusual expenses. Use plain language to explain how all fees are calculated. Disclose all fees charged and provide itemized charges if requested. Disclose average or expected fees to prospective clients.
    *   All soft dollar and bundled fees, what is received in return, and how they benefit the client.
    *   Regular and timely client investment performance reporting. Quarterly performance within 30 days of quarter end is recommended.
    *   Valuation methods used to make investment decisions and value client assets. Typical disclosure is by asset class.

- The P&Ps used for shareholder voting. These must address how controversial and unusual issues are handled, provide guidance for further actions when voting against corporate management recommendations, and disclose any delegation of voting. Provide clients details on votes cast for their holdings if requested.
- Trade allocation policies.
- Review and audit results of the client's funds and accounts.
- Significant personnel and organizational changes including mergers and acquisitions involving the firm.
- The firm's risk management process and changes to the process. Disclose what risk metrics the client will receive. Regular disclosure of client specific risk information is recommended.

KEY CONCEPTS

LOS 4.a

The purpose of AMC is to assist the firm in developing ethical business and risk management practices while gaining the trust of clients.

LOS 4.b

The AMC covers:
1. Loyalty to Clients.
2. Investment Process and Actions.
3. Trading.
4. Risk Management, Compliance, and Support.
5. Performance and Valuation.
6. Disclosures.

General principles of conduct:
- Always act ethically and professionally.
- Act in the best interest of the client.
- Act in an objective and independent manner.
- Perform actions using skill, competence, and diligence.
- Communicate accurately with clients on a regular basis.
- Comply with legal and regulatory requirements regarding capital markets.

LOS 4.c

Review the cases and work the questions in the Schweser and CFA material to practice applying the ethics requirements.

LOS 4.d

Loyalty to clients
- Always put the client's interests before your own by designing appropriate compensation arrangements for managers.
- Determine how confidential client information should be collected, utilized, and stored.
- Determine the amount of which token gifts can be accepted.

Investment process and actions
- Take reasonable care when dealing with client accounts.
- Don't engage in market manipulation.
- Deal fairly with all clients.
- Have a reasonable basis for all investment recommendations.

Trading
- Do not trade on material nonpublic information.
- Always place client trades before your own.
- Use soft dollars to aid the manager in the investment decision-making process.
- Seek best execution and allocate trades equitably among all clients.

Risk management, compliance, and support
- Ensure compliance with the Asset Manager Code and legal and regulatory requirements.
- Appoint a compliance officer.
- Disseminate portfolio information in an accurate manner.
- Have an independent third party review client accounts.
- Appropriately maintain records.
- Hire qualified staff with sufficient resources.
- Have a contingency plan in place.

Performance and valuation
- Report results in an accurate manner using fair market values.

Disclosures deal with any kind of material information disclosed to the client, such as conflicts of interest, regulatory disciplinary actions, the investment decision-making process, and strategies including inherent risks, fee schedules, calculation of performance results, proxy voting issues, allocating shares of stock, and the results of any audits.

CONCEPT CHECKERS

1. Terillium Traders is a small stock brokerage firm that specializes in buying and selling stocks on behalf of client accounts. Several of Terillium's brokers have recently been placing both a bid and an offer on the same security about two hours before the market opens for trading. This allows their trades to be one of the first ones made after the markets open. Just before the markets open, these brokers would then cancel one of the orders in anticipation that the market would move in favor of the other order. Which component, if any, of the Asset Manager Code of Professional Conduct has *most likely* been violated?
    A. The component dealing with investment process and actions related to market manipulation.
    B. The Trading section of the Code because this is an example of "front-running" client trades.
    C. Loyalty to Clients, the section pertaining to placing client interests before their own.

2. Harriet Fields, an investment adviser specializing in selling municipal bonds, advertises on television explaining the safety and security of these bonds. The bonds she is currently selling are limited obligation bonds backed only by the revenue generated from the projects they fund, which include a housing project and a golf course. Fields tells her prospective clients that the bonds are safe, secure, and offer generous interest payments. Which of the following statements is *most correct* regarding Fields's actions?
    A. Fields did not violate the Code because municipal bonds are generally regarded as being safe investments.
    B. Fields violated the part of the Code dealing with performance and valuation.
    C. Fields violated the Code when she misrepresented the bonds by not explaining their inherent risks.

3. World Investment Advisers is a large sales force of registered investment representatives which has affiliations with many firms that produce investment-related products, such as mutual funds, life insurance, mortgages, and annuities. World Investment Advisers representatives market these products to the investing public and are able to pick and choose the best products for any particular client's needs. One of the affiliated firms is a mutual fund company called Life Investors. The company has a special agreement with World Investment in which World Investment has identified Life Investors as a "preferred product provider" in their internal marketing materials to their investment representatives. In return for this preferential treatment by World Investment, Life Investors has reimbursed World Investment for the cost of these marketing materials out of the trading commissions generated from the sale of Life Investors mutual funds by World Investment sales representatives. Which of the following statements regarding any violations of the Code is *most correct*? World Investment violated the Code relating to:
    A. accepting gifts of minimal value because Life Investors is paying for the marketing materials that could influence World Investment's representatives.
    B. having a reasonable and adequate basis for making investment decisions.
    C. soft commissions by using client brokerage to pay for marketing materials.

4.   Liz Jenkins, CFA, is an asset manager for Gray Financial, a financial services firm that has adopted the Asset Manager Code in managing client accounts. Jenkins has a client who has recently been depositing into his account bearer bonds (coupon bonds) issued by Gas Tech, a natural gas exploration company. Shortly after depositing the bonds, the client has then been requesting disbursement of funds from these bonds. Jenkins suspects this client may be using the firm in an illegal money laundering scheme. Which of the following items regarding how the firm should act is *most correct*?
      A. The firm must monitor the suspicious activity without the client knowing he is being investigated.
      B. The firm must disassociate from the client.
      C. A report must be filed with the appropriate legal authorities.

5.   Kendall Asset Managers has branch offices in several different geographical locations spread out by hundreds of miles, and in some instances, located in remote areas. Due to their remote locations and small staffs, some offices do not have a compliance officer, and brokers working in these offices have sometimes had to take on the responsibility of hiring the branch manager. Some brokers work out of their homes and use their own personal e-mail to contact clients. Some branches only keep records in electronic form for seven years. Which of the following is *least likely* a breach of the Code regarding Kendall Asset Managers?
      A. Keeping records in electronic form for seven years.
      B. Communicating with clients via personal e-mail.
      C. Having the brokers in a remote office hire the branch manager.

6.   As part of the Asset Manager Code, the firm must adopt policies that:
      A. prohibit managers from engaging in outside business interests with clients separate from the portfolio management relationship.
      B. establish guidelines for when confidential client information will be disclosed to others.
      C. prohibit managers from accepting lavish gifts from clients and service providers.

For more questions related to this topic review, log in to your Schweser online account and launch SchweserPro™ QBank; and for video instruction covering each LOS in this topic review, log in to your Schweser online account and launch the OnDemand video lectures, if you have purchased these products.

ANSWERS – CONCEPT CHECKERS

1. **A**   This is an example of trying to manipulate price and/or volume. There is no indication of trying to execute for personal or firm benefit ahead of clients, making the other two choices not relevant.

2. **C**   Fields violated the Disclosures section of the Code by misrepresenting the bonds as being safe and secure. She must provide a more balanced discussion of reward and risk. Performance and valuation deals with presenting the track record of the manager and disseminating client account values to the client. Fields violated at least two of the ethical responsibilities related to the Code, which are (1) to always act in an ethical manner and (2) to act for the benefit of your clients.

3. **C**   This is a violation of the Code dealing with trading, specifically related to the use of soft dollar commissions, also referred to as client brokerage, which are trading commissions paid to World Investment by Life Investors. Soft commissions are assets of the client and should only be used to purchase goods or services to aid in the investment decision-making process (e.g., purchasing research) and should not be used to pay for marketing materials.

4. **A**   Potential illegal or unethical activity cannot be ignored. The firm must take action, such as investigating. There is no requirement to disassociate merely due to suspicion and no requirement to go to the authorities.

5. **A**   Record retention for seven years is only a suggestion if no other regulations or laws exist, but it is the least likely violation here. Using personal emails for client communication would compromise the ability to maintain and review records. Allowing the brokers to hire their supervisor would compromise any effective supervision. Communicating with clients using personal email is not acceptable because this type of communication may be difficult to monitor as mandated by the Compliance and Support part of the Code. Part of an effective compliance system is to have a designated compliance officer who can develop and implement written compliance policies. Allowing the brokers in an office to hire and presumably fire the person who is responsible for supervising them does not allow for effective internal controls, which need to be present to prevent fraudulent behavior.

6. **B**   The firm must develop policies and procedures to maintain client information, including how to deal with the rare cases it must disclose. Lavish gifts from service providers are prohibited, but not from clients. Gifts from clients are a disclosure issue. Outside business relationships with clients are not prohibited, but are another potential for conflicts of interests (like lavish client gifts), which require disclosure to the employer.

You have now finished the Ethical and Professional Standards topic section. To get immediate feedback on how effective your study has been for this material, log in to your Schweser online account and take the self-test for this topic area. Questions are more exam-like than typical Concept Checkers or QBank questions; a score of less than 70% indicates that your study likely needs improvement. These tests are timed and allow three minutes per question.

THE BEHAVIORAL FINANCE PERSPECTIVE[1]

Study Session 3

EXAM FOCUS

This opening topic review introduces the concept of behavioral finance, contrasts it with traditional finance theory, and then explores its affects on investment decision making. Behavioral finance is a relatively modern concept, and the CFA Institute introduced it into the curriculum at an early stage in the evolution of the concept. It is highly likely behavioral finance will be tested with a dedicated item set or as part of a constructed response question. In constructed response it is often linked into an investment policy statement question.

Some candidates find this study session confusing. Much of the terminology is redundant in that more than one term can mean the same thing. Many of the concepts are overlapping, and most of the questions depend heavily on comprehending the terminology. Your focus should be on understanding the basic meaning of each term as given in the material.

TRADITIONAL FINANCE VS. BEHAVIORAL FINANCE

LOS 5.a: Contrast traditional and behavioral finance perspectives on investor decision making.

Traditional finance (TF) focuses on how individuals should behave. It assumes people are rational, risk-averse, and selfish utility maximizers who act in their own self interests without regard to social values—unless such social values directly increase their own personal utility. Such individuals will act as *rational economic men*, which will lead to efficient markets where prices reflect all available, relevant information. Traditional finance is concerned with normative analysis and determining the rational solution to a problem. It uses prescriptive analysis to look for practical tools and methods to find those rational solutions.

Behavioral finance (BF) is descriptive, which focuses on describing how individuals behave and make decisions. It draws on concepts of traditional finance, psychology, and neuroeconomics. Neuroeconomics has been used to look at decision making under uncertainty, drawing on studies of brain chemistry to understand how decision making utilizes both rational and emotional areas of the brain. Behavioral finance recognizes

---

1. Terminology used throughout this topic review is industry convention as presented in Reading 5 of the 2017 CFA Level III exam curriculum.

that the way information is presented can affect decision making, leading to both emotional and cognitive biases. Individuals are *normal* and may or may not act in a risk-averse utility maximization manner. Their resulting decisions may be suboptimal from a rational (traditional finance) perspective. This can result in markets that temporarily or persistently deviate from efficiency.

Behavioral finance can be divided into two general categories: micro and macro. *Micro behavioral finance* is concerned with describing the decision-making processes of individuals. It attempts to explain why individuals deviate from traditional finance theory. *Macro behavioral finance* focuses on explaining how and why markets deviate from what we would term *efficient* in traditional finance.

Traditional Finance

Traditional finance is based on neoclassical economics and assumes individuals are risk-averse, have perfect information, and focus on maximizing their personal utility function. Investors who behave this way are then defined as rational, or a *rational economic man (REM)*. Such behavior leads to efficient markets where prices reflect available, pertinent information. A rational investor will exhibit utility theory, which asserts individuals have a limited budget and will select the mix of goods and services that maximize their utility. A rational decision maker will follow four self-evident rules or axioms:

- Completeness assumes individuals know their preferences and use them to choose between any two mutually exclusive alternatives. Given a choice between D or E, they could prefer D, E, or be indifferent.
- Transitivity assumes individuals consistently apply their completeness rankings. If D is preferred to E and F is preferred to D, then F must be preferred to E.
- Independence assumes rankings are also additive and proportional. If D and F are mutually exclusive choices where D is preferred and J is an additional choice that adds positive utility, then $D + x(J)$ will be preferred to $F + x(J)$. In this case, x is some portion of J.
- Continuity assumes utility indifference curves are continuous, meaning that unlimited combinations of weightings are possible. If F is preferred to D, which is preferred to E, then there will be a combination of F and E for which the individual will be indifferent to D.

For the Exam: Many of the assertions that are said to be self-evident under TF are not so self-evident under BF. Behavioral finance essentially asserts that this is not the way individuals always act. Most of the terminology you see here should be familiar from Levels I and II with some additions. The next section covers Bayes' formula, which was called Bayes' Theorem and posterior probabilities at Level I.

The decision process of a REM who follows these axioms can be explained using event diagrams, Bayes' formula, and updating probabilities for new information. Bayes' formula:

$$P(A \mid B) = \frac{P(B \mid A)}{P(B)} P(A)$$

where:
P(A|B) = probability of event A occurring given that event B has occurred; conditional probability of event A
P(B|A) = probability of event B occurring given that event A has occurred; conditional probability of event B
P(B)   = unconditional probability of event B occurring
P(A)   = unconditional probability of event A occurring

Example: Applying Bayes' formula

Assume a blue bag and a green bag each contain 10 coins:

* The blue bag contains 4 U.S. coins and 6 Canadian coins.
* The green bag contains 8 U.S. coins and 2 Canadian coins.

Without looking at the bags, a young boy reaches into one of them and withdraws a U.S. coin. Determine the probability that the boy reached into the blue bag.

Answer:

The first step is to draw the event diagram.

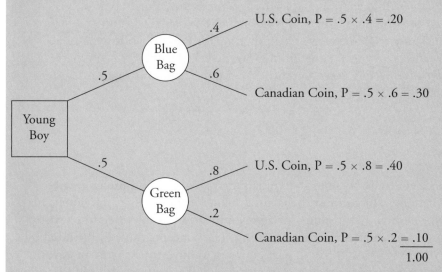

* Each bag contains 10 coins for a total of 20 coins. The probability of any single coin coming from either the blue or green bag is 10/20 = .5.
* The probability of withdrawing a U.S. coin from the blue bag is 4 out of 10 = 40%.
* The probability if withdrawing a U.S. coin from the green bag is 8 out of 10 = 80%.

If it was not known a U.S. coin had been drawn, then the probability the blue bag was selected would be 50% as there were only two choices. However, knowing a U.S. coin was drawn allows the probabilities to be updated for this information. Knowing a U.S. coin was pulled from a bag, what is the probability the boy reached into the blue bag? The answer is the probability of selecting a U.S. coin from the blue bag (.5 × .4 = .20) over the total probability that a U.S. coin would be selected from either bag (.40 + .20 = .60) for a probability of .20/.60 = 33.3%. Using the equation, it is:

$$P(A\mid B) = \frac{P(B\mid A)}{P(B)}P(A) = \frac{40\%}{60\%}(50\%) = 33.3\%$$

where:
P(A|B) = probability that the blue bag was selected given that the boy withdrew a U.S. coin (to be determined)
P(B|A) = probability of withdrawing a U.S. coin given that the blue bag was selected = 40%
P(B) = probability of withdrawing a U.S. coin = 60%
P(A) = probability of selecting the blue bag = 50%

For the Exam: A Level III candidate developed a study plan six months before the exam after carefully considering their personal strengths and weaknesses, their available study time, and the exam weight of each topic. It is now three weeks prior to the exam and, as often happens, the candidate is behind on the study plan. The candidate becomes even more determined to complete the original study plan.

It could be said the candidate is failing to adjust probability weights for new information. The new information is that the remaining time to study is only three weeks, and the original study plan is no longer optimal. The candidate has not updated the study schedule to weigh study time for the probability material is important on the exam and for the limited three weeks of study time available. Subsequent BF concepts will also suggest the candidate is committing numerous cognitive and emotional errors to the candidate's detriment.

RISK AVERSION

Traditional finance generally assumes individuals are risk-averse and prefer greater certainty to less certainty. In contrast, behavioral finance assumes that individuals may be risk-averse, risk-neutral, risk-seeking, or any combination of the three; the way something is presented can affect decision making. The concepts can be illustrated by considering what a person would pay to participate in an investment with an equal probability of the investment paying back immediately GBP 100 or GBP 200. In other words, it would pay back on average GBP150.

Risk-averse. The risk-averse person suffers a greater loss of utility for a given loss of wealth than they gain in utility for the same rise in wealth. Therefore, they would pay less than GBP 150 for an uncertain, but expected, payoff of GBP 150.

Risk-neutral. The risk-neutral person gains or loses the same utility for a given gain or loss of wealth and would be willing to pay GBP 150 for the expected payoff of GBP 150.

Risk seeker. The risk-seeking person gains more in utility for a rise in wealth than they lose in utility for an equivalent fall in wealth. Therefore, they would pay more than GBP 150.

In each case, the person's utility (satisfaction) is a function of wealth and can be described graphically.

Figure 1: Utility Function of Wealth

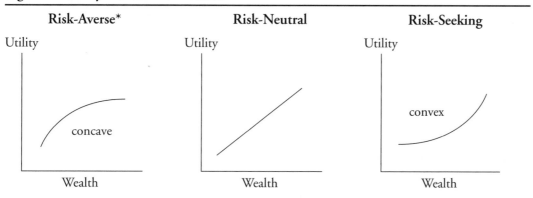

* Generally assumed for Traditional Finance Theory

Challenges to Traditional Finance and the Rational Economic Man

Behavioral finance does not assume individuals are always risk-averse, that they adhere to Bayes' formula, that they act in their own self-interest, or that they have perfect information. Individuals sometimes act as rational economic men (REM), but at other times, their behavior is better explained by psychology. Challenges to REM include:

- Decision making can be flawed by lack of information or flaws in the decision-making process.
- Personal inner conflicts that prioritize short-term (spending) goals over long-term (saving) goals can lead to poor prioritization.
- Lack of perfect knowledge is perhaps the most serious challenge to REM. How many individuals can properly assess the impacts of a change in central bank policy on their future wealth?
- Wealth utility functions may not always be concave as assumed by utility theory, and individuals can sometimes exhibit risk seeking behavior.

UTILITY THEORY AND PROSPECT THEORY

LOS 5.b: Contrast expected utility and prospect theories of investment decision making.

For the Exam: This material is very theoretical, and it is not always clear in the reading exactly what could be relevant to any particular LOS. You would be wise to work through the end-of-chapter questions for the CFA readings to get a better sense of what level of detail is expected.

Utility Theory and Indifference Curves

Traditional finance is based in **utility theory** with an assumption of diminishing marginal return. This leads to two consequences. First, the risk-averse utility function is concave. As more and more wealth is added, utility (satisfaction) increases at a diminishing rate. Second, it leads to convex indifference curves due to a diminishing marginal rate of substitution.

For example, consider an individual looking at the trade-off between paid hours of work (W) and unpaid hours of leisure (L). Suppose an individual has 12 hours available in a day after allowing for sleep, eating, and other needs. How would the individual split work hours and leisure hours to maintain an indifferent level of satisfaction?

- Suppose the individual currently works 11 hours with 1 hour of leisure. Having little leisure time, the individual might trade 5W for 3L, a 5/3 trade-off, that results in a total of 6W and 4L at the same level of satisfaction.
- From the new indifference point, adding more leisure adds less marginal utility. The individual might only give up 5 more W for 7L, a 5/7 trade-off, resulting in 1W and 11L.
- At any point on the indifference curve, they are equally satisfied.

Figure 2: Trade-Off between Work and Leisure

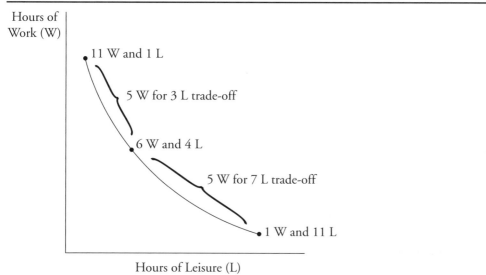

Hours of Work (W)

- 11 W and 1 L
- 5 W for 3 L trade-off
- 6 W and 4 L
- 5 W for 7 L trade-off
- 1 W and 11 L

Hours of Leisure (L)

While indifference curves and utility theory appear rational, they ignore that many individuals are unable to quantify such mathematical trade-offs. Indifference curves also don't explicitly consider risk and the assumption of risk aversion. For example, during recessions when jobs are scarce, the trade-off of W for L would likely change.

Complex Risk Functions

Behavioral finance observes that individuals sometimes exhibit risk-seeking as well as risk-averse behavior. Many people simultaneously purchase low-payoff, low-risk insurance policies (risk-averse behavior) and low-probability, high-payoff lottery tickets (risk-seeking behavior). Combinations of risk seeking and risk aversion may result in a complex double inflection utility function.

Figure 3: Friedman-Savage, Double-Inflextion Utility Function

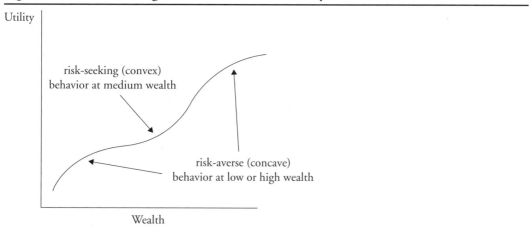

Utility

risk-seeking (convex) behavior at medium wealth

risk-averse (concave) behavior at low or high wealth

Wealth

Decision Theory

Decision theory is focused on making the ideal decision when the decision maker is fully informed, mathematically able, and rational. The theory has evolved over time.

- Initial analysis focused on selecting the highest probability-weighted payoff.
- Later evolution separated expected value, which is just the market price of an item paid by anyone versus expected utility. Expected utility is subjective and depends on the unique preferences of individuals and their unique rate of diminishing marginal utility and substitution.
- Risk is defined as a random variable due to the one outcome that will occur from any probability-weighted analysis. For example, a stock has an expected return denoted $E(R)$ of 10% but returns 12%. Risk can be incorporated into analysis by maximizing expected utility.
- In contrast, uncertainty is unknowable outcomes and probabilities. It is, by definition, immeasurable and not amenable to traditional utility maximization analysis.
- Subjective analysis extends decision theory to situations where probability cannot be objectively measured but is subjective.

LOS 5.c: Discuss the effect that cognitive limitations and bounded rationality may have on investment decision making.

In traditional finance, all investors are assumed to possess the same information and interpret it accurately and instantly, without bias, in evaluating investments and in making utility-maximizing decisions. Behavioral finance acknowledges that investors do not always make decisions consistent with this form of utility maximization.

Bounded Rationality

Bounded rationality assumes knowledge capacity limits and removes the assumptions of perfect information, fully rational decision making, and consistent utility maximization. Individuals instead practice satisfice. Outcomes that offer sufficient satisfaction, but not optimal utility, are sufficient.

 Professor's Note: Cognitive limitations stem from a lack of the resources, mental or mechanical, to thoroughly interpret information. Knowledge limitations refer to the inability to have all relevant information.

Example: Satisfice and bounded rationality

Jane Smith has excess funds she can deposit to earn interest. She wants the funds to be backed by the government, so she visits the bank closest to her workplace. The rate seems acceptable, and she makes the deposit after verifying that the deposits are government insured. Is her behavior consistent with a rational economic man?

Answer:

No. Smith is showing bounded rationality and satisfice. The rate was adequate and met the condition of government guarantee, so she accepted it. She did not research all other options or have perfect information (bounded rationality). There is no reason to expect that this particular rate is the optimal solution.

Prospect Theory

For the Exam: The LOS and end-of-chapter questions are conceptually focused and not mathematically focused. The discussion of the evaluation phase of prospect theory specifically says "a quantitative illustration … is complex and not necessary to review here." No math is provided.

Bounded rationality relaxes the assumptions of perfect information and maximizing expected utility. Prospect theory further relaxes the assumption of risk aversion and instead proposes loss aversion. Prospect theory is suited to analyzing investment decisions and risk. It focuses on the framing of decisions as either gains or losses and weighting uncertain outcomes. While utility theory assumes risk aversion, prospect theory assumes loss aversion.

Under prospect theory, choices are made in two phases. In the first phase, the editing phase, proposals are framed or edited using simple heuristics (decision rules) to make a preliminary analysis prior to the second evaluation phase. In the editing phase, economically identical outcomes are grouped and a reference point is established to rank the proposals. The goal of the editing phase is to simplify the number of choices that must be made before making the final evaluation and decision. Doing so addresses the cognitive limitations individuals face in evaluating large amounts of information. The risk is that the selection of the reference point frames the proposal as a gain or loss and affects the subsequent evaluation or decision step.

In the second phase, the evaluation phase, investors focus on loss aversion rather than risk aversion. The difference is subtle, but the implication is that investors are more concerned with the *change in wealth* than they are in the resulting level of wealth, per se. In addition, investors are assumed to place a greater value in change on a loss than on a gain of the same amount. Given a potential loss and gain of equal sizes, the increase in utility associated with the potential gain is smaller than the decrease in utility (i.e., disutility) associated with the potential loss. Investors tend to fear losses and can become risk seeking (assume riskier positions) in an attempt to avoid them.

Experiments have shown that most individuals will not take a gamble that offers 50/50 odds of equal but opposite payoffs. For example, the average individual will not take a gamble with 50% probability of winning $100 and 50% probability of losing $100, even though the expected outcome is $0. The possible gain would have to be increased to at least $200 (at least double the possible loss) to entice the average individual to take the gamble.

Example: Framing the decision as a gain or loss

Portfolio Assets	Current Price	Cost Basis	Yesterday's Close	Year-end Close
A	10	7	11	9
B	12	13	13	13
C	14	9	15	13

Which asset has the largest percentage loss?

Answer:

It depends on the selected (framed) reference point to determine perceived loss. A perception can affect subsequent decisions. For example, if yesterday's close is the reference point, every asset has a perceived loss with Asset A having the largest percentage loss. However, if cost basis is the selected reference, then B has the largest percentage loss while A and C have gains.

Editing Phase

The early editing phase can involve a large number of operations. The precise sequence and number of steps is determined by the data. The first three steps may apply to individual proposals.

1. **Codification** codes the proposal as a gain or loss of value and assigns a probability to each possible outcome. To do this, the reference point must be selected.

2. **Combination** simplifies the outcomes by combining those with identical values. For example, an investor might probability weight expected returns of a stock (codification) and then combine identical outcomes.

Figure 4: Example of Combination

Outcomes:		Combined Outcomes:	
Probability (p)	E(R)	Probability (p)	E(R)
.10	−5%	.10	−5%
.20	0%	.20	0%
.20	10%		
.30	10%	.50	10%
.20	20%	.20	20%
1.00		1.00	

3. **Segregation** can be used to separate an expected return into both a risk-free and risky component of return. For example, assume a gamble offers a 75% chance of a $100 payoff and a 25% chance of paying $150. This can be segregated as a 100% risk-free payoff of $100 and a 25% chance of another $50.

The next three steps may apply when comparing two or more proposals.

4. **Cancellation** removes any outcomes common to two proposals. Overlapping outcomes would not affect any decision.

Figure 5: Example of Cancelation

	Before Cancelation:			*After Cancelation:*		
Proposal A:						
E(R)	5%	10%	15%			15%
p	.333	.333	.333			.333
Proposal B:						
E(R)	5%	10%		5%	10%	
p	.50	.50		.167	.167	

5. **Simplification** applies to very small differences in probabilities or to highly unlikely outcomes. For example, a 49% chance of $500 with a 50% chance of $700 and a 1% chance of $750 might be simplified as an equal chance of $500 or $700.

6. **Detection of dominance** would discard from consideration any proposal that is clearly dominated. The previous 50/50 chance of $500 or $700 dominates an equal chance of $400 or $600 in every regard: higher average, higher minimum, and higher maximum.

Editing choices can sometimes lead to the preference anomaly known as the **isolation effect**, where investors focus on one factor or outcome while consciously eliminating or subconsciously ignoring others. It is referred to as an anomaly because the sequence of the editing can lead to different decisions.

Example: The isolation effect

Assume an individual is asked to choose between two lotteries:

- Lottery 1 offers payoffs of a 33% chance of $3,000 or nothing.
- Lottery 2 offers payoffs of a 20% chance of $5,500 or nothing.

The expected (probability weighted) payoffs are $1,000 and $1,100 respectively.

Not surprisingly empirical studies show that most individuals select the higher and rational payoff of Lottery 2.

However, framing the lottery (e.g., changing the order of presentation) can affect the selection. Suppose the expected payoffs of Lottery 1 and Lottery 2 in this case were maintained, but they were recast to occur in the second stage of a two-stage lottery. In the new game, the first stage has a 67% chance in ending in a zero payoff and a 33% chance of moving on to the second stage. The second stage will consist of either Lottery 3 or Lottery 4, but an individual must select to participate in either Lottery 3 or Lottery 4 before the first stage is played. In other words, it is not known if the individual has moved to the second stage before selecting Lottery 3 or Lottery 4. They do know that:

- Lottery 3 offers payoffs of a 100% chance of $3,000 or nothing.
- Lottery 4 offers payoffs of a 60% chance of $5,500 or nothing.

What is surprising is that a majority of individuals now choose Lottery 3 even though it has an expected payoff of $1,000 versus $1,100 for Lottery 4. This is the opposite of the choice made when confronted with choosing between Lottery 1 and Lottery 2.

Expected payoffs:

Lottery 1: .33 × $3,000 ≈ $1,000

Lottery 2: .20 × $5,500 = $1,100

Lottery 3: .33 × 1.00 × $3,000 ≈ $1,000

Lottery 4: .33 × .60 × $5,500 ≈ $1,100

Empirical studies have shown the framing and order of the lottery can produce inconsistent and irrational choices.

 Professor's Note: Please do not send in emails saying the calculations above are not precise. The ≈ sign was used intentionally, and the calculations are demonstrating the simplification step.

The Evaluation Phase

In the **evaluation phase**, investors place values on alternatives in terms of weighted and probability-weighted outcome to determine expected utility. A quantitative illustration is complex and specifically stated to be unnecessary to the purpose of the reading (thus, it is not presented here). The equation is shown as:

$$\text{utility} = w(p_1)v(X_1) + w(p_2)v(X_2) + \dots$$

where:
p_1 and p_2 = probability weights of possible outcomes X_1 and X_2
v = a function that assigns value to an outcome
w = a probability weighting function

The important implications are:

- *w* reflects a tendency of individuals to overreact to small probabilities and underreact to large probabilities.
- The value function is based on changes and is not level.
- The resulting value function is S-shaped and asymmetric. Individuals experience a greater decline in value for a given loss than a rise in value for a corresponding gain.

Figure 6: Value Function

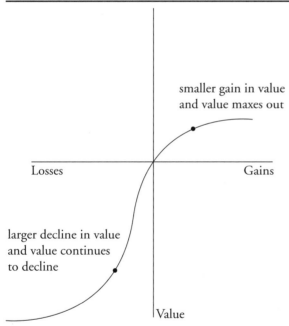

- As a result, most investors are risk averse when presented with gains. Empirical studies show that when given an equal chance of making $100 or losing $70, most individuals will not take the bet. They are risk averse and want a higher expected payoff than $15.
- However, most individuals are risk seekers when confronted with likely losses. Offered the choice of a sure loss of $75 or a 50/50 chance of winning $30 or losing $200, they exhibit risk-seeking behavior by taking the bet that has an expected payoff of –$85. The bet is worse than the sure loss of $75.
- This could explain why many investors over-concentrate in high-risk and low-risk investments but not medium-risk investments.

Figure 7: Summary of Traditional Finance versus Bounded Rationality and Prospect Theory

Traditional Finance Assumes:	*Bounded Rationality* and Prospect Theory** Assume:*
Unlimited perfect knowledge	Capacity limitations on knowledge*
Utility maximization	Satisfice*
Fully rational decision making	Cognitive limits on decision making*
Risk aversion	Reference dependence to determine gain or loss leading to possible cognitive errors**

CAPITAL MARKETS AND PORTFOLIO CONSTRUCTION

LOS 5.d: Compare traditional and behavioral finance perspectives on portfolio construction and the behavior of capital markets.

The Traditional Finance Perspective

Much of modern portfolio theory is premised on the *efficient market hypothesis* (EMH). The EMH presumes market prices reflect all relevant available information. The aggregate decision making of market participants is correct even if individual investors are wrong. The resulting efficient prices reflect intrinsic value and do not allow investors to earn excess, risk-adjusted returns after allowing for transaction costs. The EMH proposes three versions of efficiency:

- A market is **weak-form efficient** if current prices incorporate all past price and volume data. If markets are weakly efficient, managers cannot consistently generate excess returns using technical analysis (charting).
- If a market is **semi-strong form efficient**, prices reflect all public information, including past price and volume data. The moment valuable information is released, it is fully and accurately reflected in asset prices. If markets are semi-strong form efficient, managers cannot consistently generate excess returns using technical or fundamental analysis.
- **Strong-form efficiency** requires prices to reflect all privileged nonpublic (i.e., inside) information as well as all public information, including past price and volume data. If a market is strong-form efficient, no analysis based on inside and/or public information can consistently generate excess returns. Strong-form efficiency is not generally accepted as nonpublic information is associated with excess returns.

Support for the EMH

The weak form of the EMH has been the most studied and supported. If past security prices show strong serial correlation, then past prices could be used to predict subsequent changes. Nevertheless, historical studies show virtually zero serial correlation, which is consistent with weak-form efficiency. Stock price changes appear random.

However, the random nature of stock prices does not by itself support the further notion that the *price is right* and that price correctly reflects intrinsic value. Accepting the price as right when it does not, in fact, reflect intrinsic value could lead to a serious misallocation of portfolio resources.

Tests of the semi-strong form have focused on two areas:

- Event studies, such as the announcement of a stock split, look for evidence that such events are predictive of future stock price movement. In itself, a stock split creates no economic value and should not affect the split adjusted price. However, splits are strongly associated with abnormal dividend increases that might reflect rising economic value. Event studies show that stock prices rise abnormally for up to two years before the split and complete an upward adjustment coincident with the split announcement. This is consistent with the semi-strong EMH. Of course, if you knew ahead of time that the split and dividend increases were coming, it would allow you to earn excess returns. The ability to benefit from advance inside information is consistent with semi-strong form but is a rejection of strong-form efficiency.
- Other studies focus on the aggregate ability of professional managers to generate positive excess return or alpha. Studies of mutual fund managers show the majority have negative alphas both before and after management fees. This is consistent with semi-strong EMH. This is sometimes referred to as *no free lunch*, which asserts that it is difficult or impossible to consistently outperform on a risk-adjusted basis.

Challenges to EMH

Some studies do find evidence that appears to be or is inconsistent with the EMH. If such market anomalies persist, those anomalies argue for inefficiency of markets. Several different forms of anomalies have been identified.

Fundamental anomalies would relate future stock returns to stock fundamentals, such as P/E or dividend yield. Fundamental anomalies would be violations of both semi-strong and strong-form efficiency.

Numerous studies have shown evidence that value stocks with lower P/E, P/B, and P/S, higher E/P and B/P, and dividend yield outperform growth stocks (which tend to have the opposite fundamental characteristics).

Studies show abnormal positive returns for small-cap stocks.

Other studies suggest the abnormal return of value stocks is not evidence of excess return but of higher risk. Fama and French (1995, 2008) propose extending the capital asset pricing model (CAPM) to include market cap and B/P as priced risks. Analysis using these revised risk premiums suggests the apparent excess returns are just a failure to properly adjust (upward) for risk.

> **For the Exam:** This discussion is a perfect example of the kind of material you will commonly see at Level III. You could be asked to discuss evidence that contradicts the EMH and then to critique that same evidence. You are expected to understand both sides of the issue when the material is well discussed in the curriculum. Your general conclusion should be that markets are mostly efficient but with exceptions.

Technical anomalies relate to studies of past stock price and volume. Technical anomalies would be violations of all three forms of efficiency. (Hint: Remember the semi-strong and strong forms encompass the weak form as well.)

- Studies have shown that when a short-term (1-, 2-, or 5-day) moving average of price moves above (below) a longer-term (50-, 150-, or 200-day) moving average, it signals a buy (sell). Other studies show that when a stock price rises above a resistance level, it signals a buy; if the stock price moves below a support level, it signals a sell. As such, the signals do provide value.

Calendar anomalies appear to show that stocks (small-cap stocks in particular) have abnormally high returns in January, in the last day of each month, and in the first four days of each month. The January anomaly has been known and studied for more than 25 years but has persisted. It would be a violation of all forms of EMH.

Even when an anomaly may appear to violate the EMH, there may be no outperformance when transaction costs and risks are considered. Alternatively, any benefits may be temporary and the anomaly may disappear as investors buy and sell securities to exploit the opportunity. On the other hand, limits to arbitrage activity may allow anomalies to persist.

The ability of investors to withdraw funds from a manager may limit arbitrage activity. An arbitrageur takes positions in anticipation those prices will correct, often using high leverage. For example, the arbitrageur could take a position to exploit the January effect, buying a stock in anticipation of the rise. If prices do not move up as quickly as expected, the arbitrageur's investors may become dissatisfied and withdraw funds. The arbitrageur must then sell, pushing down the stock price, which is the opposite of what was expected. Such liquidity issues may put limits on the ability of arbitrage to establish market efficiency. A highly leveraged arbitrageur must be correct and market prices must correct quickly and in the way expected.

The Behavioral Finance Perspective

Traditional finance (TF) assumes markets are efficient and prices reflect fundamental value. New information is quickly and properly reflected in market prices. Portfolio managers can focus on identifying efficient portfolios on the efficient frontier that meet the client's objectives of risk and return while also observing the investor's constraints. (These ideas of portfolio management will be extensively covered in later study sessions.) However, if prices are not correctly reflecting intrinsic value, or at least providing the best indication possible, this approach to portfolio management is flawed.

Behavioral finance (BF) challenges these traditional finance notions. It has not yet been able to propose a unified, alternative theory. Four alternative behavioral models have been proposed: (1) consumption and savings, (2) behavioral asset pricing, (3) behavioral portfolio theory, and (4) the adaptive markets hypothesis.

For the Exam: The previous section on TF, along with a conceptual understanding of the four alternative models that follows, is the most direct answer to LOS 5.d.

1. **Consumption and savings:** Traditional finance assumes investors are able to save and invest in the earlier stages of life to fund later retirement. This requires investors to show self control by delaying short-term spending gratification to meet long-term goals. The consumption and savings approach proposes an alternative *behavioral life-cycle model* that questions the ability to exercise self control and suggests individuals instead show mental accounting and framing biases. Investors mentally account and frame wealth as current income, assets currently owned, and present value of future income.

   Traditional finance assumes that all forms of wealth are interchangeable. Behavioral finance presumes the mental accounting for wealth by source makes individuals less likely to spend from current assets and expected future wages. Therefore, individuals will overcome at least some of their lack of self-control to save some of what they will need to meet long-term goals. This also makes them subject to framing bias. For example, if individuals perceive a bonus as current income, they are more likely to spend it. If they perceive it as future income, they are more likely to save it.

2. **Behavioral asset pricing:** Traditional asset pricing models (e.g., CAPM) assume market prices are determined through an unbiased analysis of risk and return. The intrinsic value of an asset is its expected cash flows discounted at a required return, based on the risk-free rate and a fundamental risk premium. The behavioral asset pricing model adds a **sentiment premium**[2] to the discount rate; the required return on an asset is the risk-free rate, plus a fundamental risk premium, plus a sentiment premium. The sentiment premium can be estimated by considering the dispersion of analysts' forecasts. A high dispersion suggests a higher sentiment premium.

   Under the traditional CAPM, the sentiment premium would be unwarranted. If this added, erroneous error is systematic and predictable, it might be possible to exploit it. If it is random, it will be more difficult to exploit.

For the Exam: The reading does not elaborate on this point, but consider the earlier discussion of arbitrage. If a price can be identified as wrong and is expected to quickly correct, it can be exploited to earn excess profit. If it just stays wrong, the arbitrage does not work.

---

2. The sentiment premium is referred to as a **stochastic discount factor** (SDF) in the proposed asset pricing model and is based on investor sentiment relative to fundamental value. Shefrin, Hersh, and Meir Statman, 1994. "Behavioral Capital Asset Pricing Theory." *Journal of Financial and Quantitative Analysis*, vol. 35, no. 2.

3. **Behavioral portfolio theory (BPT):** Based on empirical evidence and observation, rather than hold a well-diversified portfolio as prescribed by traditional finance, individuals construct a portfolio by layers. Each layer reflects a different expected return and risk. BPT further asserts that individuals tend to concentrate their holdings in nearly risk-free or much riskier assets. Allocation of funds to an investment of each layer depends on:

   - The importance of each goal to the investor. If a high return for the goal is important, funds will be allocated to the high-return (high-risk) layer. If low risk is crucial to the goal, funds will be allocated to the low-risk (low-return) layer.
   - Asset selection will be done by layer and based on the goal for that layer. If high return is the goal, then higher-risk, more-speculative assets will be selected.
   - The number of assets in a layer will reflect the investor's risk aversion. Risk-averse investors with a concave utility function will hold larger numbers of assets in each layer.
   - If an investor believes they hold an information advantage (have information others do not have), more concentrated positions will be held.
   - If an investor is loss-averse, the investor will hold larger cash positions to avoid the possible need to sell assets at a loss to meet liquidity needs.

   The resulting overall portfolio may appear to be diversified but is likely to be sub-optimal because the layers were constructed without regard to their correlation with each other. Such layering can explain:

   - The irrational holding of both insurance, a low risk asset, and high-risk lottery tickets by the same individual.
   - Holding excess cash and low-risk bonds in the low-risk layer and excessively risky assets in the high-risk layer. (This also includes not holding more moderate-risk assets.)

4. **Adaptive markets hypothesis (AMH):** The AMH assumes successful market participants apply heuristics until they no longer work and then adjust them accordingly. In other words, success in the market is an evolutionary process. Those who do not or cannot adapt do not survive.

   Because AMH is based on behavioral finance theory, it assumes investors satisfice rather than maximize utility. Based on an amount of information they feel is sufficient, they make decisions to reach subgoals, steps that advance them toward their desired goal. In this fashion, they do not necessarily make optimal decisions as prescribed by utility theory or act as REM. Through trial and error, these heuristic rules that work come to be adopted by more and more participants until they are reflected in market pricing and then no longer work. The market evolves.

   AMH leads to five conclusions:

   - The relationship of risk and return should not be stable. The market risk premium changes over time as the competitive environment changes.
   - Active management can find opportunities to exploit arbitrage and add value.
   - No strategy should work all the time.
   - Adaption and innovation are essential to continued success.
   - Survivors change and adapt.

AMH is essentially EMH with bounded rationality, satisficing, and evolution. In AMH, the degree to which the market is efficient will depend on the degree of competition in the market, the availability of profit, and the flexibility of participants to exploit opportunity.

Hopefully, in time, the insights of behavioral finance will allow for the construction of portfolios that are efficient from a traditional finance perspective and understandable to investors. If an investor can understand the portfolio, the investor is more likely to stay with it for the long run.

KEY CONCEPTS

LOS 5.a

Traditional finance is *prescriptive*; it explains how investors *should* make investment decisions based on mathematical models and theories. Behavioral finance is *descriptive*; it tries to explain *observed* investor decision making.

To maximize utility, a rational investor will make decisions conforming to the four axioms of utility: completeness, transitivity, independence, and continuity.

With the receipt of new, relevant information, rational investors revise expectations utilizing a Bayesian framework.

LOS 5.b

Traditional finance is based in utility theory and an assumption of diminishing marginal return. This leads to two consequences. First, the risk-averse utility function is concave. As more and more wealth is added, utility (satisfaction) increases at a diminishing rate. Second, it leads to convex indifference curves due to a diminishing marginal rate of substitution.

Decision theory is focused on making the ideal decision when the decision maker is fully informed, mathematically able, and rational. The theory has evolved over time.
- Initial analysis focused on selecting the highest probability-weighted payoff.
- Later evolution separated expected value, which is just the market price of an item paid by anyone, from expected utility. Expected utility is subjective and depends on the unique preferences of individuals and their unique rate of diminishing marginal utility and substitution.
- Risk is defined as a random variable due to the one outcome that will occur from any probability-weighted analysis. For example, a stock has an E(R) of 10% but returns 12%. Risk can be incorporated into analysis by maximizing expected utility.
- In contrast, uncertainty is unknowable outcomes and probabilities. It is, by definition, immeasurable and not amenable to traditional utility maximization analysis.
- Subjective analysis extends decision theory to situations where probability cannot be objectively measured but is subjective.

LOS 5.c

Bounded rationality means that individuals act as rationally as possible, given their lack of knowledge and lack of cognitive ability.

Rather than optimize, individuals satisfice. Investors gather what they consider to be an adequate amount of information and apply heuristics to arrive at an acceptable decision. The result is that the investor takes steps and accepts short-term goals toward the ultimately desired goal. The investor does not necessarily make the theoretically optimal decision from a tradition finance perspective.

LOS 5.d

Traditional finance (TF) assumes markets are efficient and prices reflect fundamental value. New information is quickly and properly reflected in market prices. Portfolio managers can focus on identifying efficient portfolios on the efficient frontier that met the client's objectives of risk and return while observing the investor's constraints. (These ideas of portfolio management will be extensively covered in later study sessions.) However, if prices are not correctly reflecting intrinsic value, or at least providing the best indication possible, this approach to portfolio management is flawed.

Behavioral finance (BF) challenges these TF notions. However, it has not yet been able to propose a unified, alternative theory. Four alternative behavioral models have been proposed: (1) consumption and savings, (2) behavioral asset pricing, (3) behavioral portfolio theory, and (4) the adaptive markets hypothesis.

1. **Consumption and savings approach:** Traditional finance assumes investors are able to save and invest in the earlier stages of life to fund later retirement. The consumption and savings approach proposes an alternative *behavioral life-cycle model* that questions the ability to exercise self control and suggests individuals instead show mental accounting and framing biases.

2. **Behavioral asset pricing:** Traditional asset pricing models (e.g., CAPM) assume market prices are determined through an unbiased analysis of risk and return. The intrinsic value of an asset is its expected cash flows discounted at a required return, based on the risk-free rate and a fundamental risk premium. The behavioral asset pricing model adds a **sentiment premium** to the discount rate; the required return on an asset is the risk-free rate, plus a fundamental risk premium, plus a sentiment premium. Under the traditional CAPM, the sentiment premium would be unwarranted.

3. **Behavioral portfolio theory (BPT):** Based on empirical evidence and observation, rather than hold a well-diversified portfolio as prescribed by traditional finance, individuals construct a portfolio by layers. Each layer reflects a different expected return and risk. BPT further asserts that individuals tend to concentrate their holdings in nearly risk-free and much riskier assets. Allocation of funds to and investment of each layer depends on the importance of each goal to the investor. If a high return for the goal is important funds will be allocated to the high return (high risk) layer in the form of more speculative assets. If low risk is crucial to the goal then funds will be allocated to the low risk (low return layer) in the form of larger cash positions and low risk bonds. Risk-averse investors with a concave utility function will hold larger numbers of assets in each layer. If an investor believes they hold an information advantage (have information others do not have) more concentrated positions will be held.

4. **Adaptive markets hypothesis (AMH):** The AMH assumes successful market participants apply heuristics until they no longer work and then adjust them accordingly. In other words, success in the market is an evolutionary process. Those who do not or cannot adapt do not survive. AMH assumes investors satisfice rather than maximize utility.

CONCEPT CHECKERS

1. An investor has ranked three investments and labeled them as A, B, and C. He prefers investment A to investment B and investment B to investment C. Not being able to rank investment A relative to investment C would *most likely* violate which of the four axioms of utility?
    A. Continuity.
    B. Dominance.
    C. Transitivity.

2. Applying the independence axiom of utility, an investor who prefers investment A to investment B and has the option to add all or a portion of investment C to his selection would **NOT** prefer:
    A. (A + C) to (B + C).
    B. (A + 0.25C) to (B + 0.25C).
    C. (B + 0.75C) to (A + 0.75C).

3. Data for two investments are presented below:

Investment	Expected Return	Standard Deviation
A	8%	20%
B	10%	20%

    A rational investor who selects investment B over investment A would *most likely* have a utility function characterized as:
    A. concave.
    B. convex.
    C. linear.

4. An investor who actively seeks risk in investing *most likely* experiences:
    A. constant marginal utility.
    B. decreasing marginal utility.
    C. increasing marginal utility.

5. According to prospect theory, investors are more concerned with changes in wealth than in returns, per se. Prospect theory suggests that investors:
    A. are risk averse.
    B. can be loss averse.
    C. place more value on gains than on losses of equal magnitude.

6. Based on the following data, **determine** and **explain** using expected utility whether or not the investor is likely to make the investment.

Outcome	Utility	Probability of Occurrence	Subjective Probability Factor
–8%	–120	15%	1.25
0%	–10	40%	1.15
6%	50	30%	0.85
10%	100	15%	0.65
Total	20	100%	

7. At lunch, two portfolio managers discuss their recent trades. One complains that it is extremely difficult if not impossible to gather and analyze all relevant available information before trading. He admits that he often just "goes with" the information he has. **Determine** the behavioral bias most likely indicated by his actions and **explain** your choice.

8. Satisficing is *best* described as:
   A. making short-term, suboptimal decisions.
   B. making utility-maximizing decisions.
   C. a form of bounded rationality that causes investors to act rationally.

9. Two analysts are overheard discussing market efficiency. They make the following statements:

"I don't care who you are. If the stock market is semi-strong efficient, no information can consistently generate excess returns. There are no free lunches!"

"The January effect supports the assertion that markets are not strong-form efficient."

Determine whether you agree or disagree with each statement, and if you disagree, justify your decision with one reason. Answer in the template provided.

Statement	Agree/Disagree	Justification
"I don't care who you are. If the stock market is semi-strong efficient, no information can consistently generate excess returns. There are no free lunches!"	Agree Disagree	
"The January effect supports the assertion that markets are not strong-form efficient."	Agree Disagree	

10. Two analysts are overheard discussing technical trading rules. One says, "I have noticed over the last year or so that the market rises to about 11,000 and then falls back. It seems to do that every two to three months. At the bottom, it goes to about 10,000 and then rebounds. It's sort of like watching a roller coaster." From a technical standpoint, the numbers 10,000 and 11,000 in the analyst's statement would *most likely* be referred to respectively as:
    A. a fundamental anomaly and a technical anomaly.
    B. a support and a resistance level.
    C. both would be considered fundamental anomalies.

11. Two analysts are overheard discussing technical trading rules. One says, "I have noticed over the last year or so that the market rises to about 11,000 and then falls back. It seems to do that every two to three months. At the bottom, it goes to about 10,000 and then rebounds. It's sort of like watching a roller coaster."

    The market consistently staying in a band between 10,000 and 11,000 is *most likely* to be used as evidence against which form of market efficiency?
    A. Weak-form efficient.
    B. Semi-strong form efficient.
    C. Strong-form efficient.

12.   An analyst states that investors should not conclude that market prices do not fully reflect all public information simply because they can temporarily wander from their intrinsic values. Use a liquidity argument to **explain** why the analyst is correct.

13.   Beth Smargen, CFA candidate, makes the following statement:

        "The behavioral asset pricing model incorporates a sentiment premium when valuing assets. For example, the more strongly analysts feel about a security, the greater the sentiment premium and the higher the price."

        In the template, **indicate** by circling whether you agree or disagree with Smargen's statement. If you disagree, **justify** your decision.

Statement	Agree/Disagree	Justification
"The behavioral asset pricing model incorporates a sentiment premium when valuing assets. For example, the more strongly analysts feel about a security, the greater the sentiment premium and the higher the price."	Agree Disagree	

For more questions related to this topic review, log in to your Schweser online account and launch SchweserPro™ QBank; and for video instruction covering each LOS in this topic review, log in to your Schweser online account and launch the OnDemand video lectures, if you have purchased these products.

ANSWERS – CONCEPT CHECKERS

1. **C** According to transitivity, investment rankings must be applied consistently. If an investor prefers investment A to investment B and prefers investment B to investment C, he must prefer investment A to investment C. Continuity is the axiom of utility that must apply for indifference curves to be smooth and unbroken (continuous). Dominance has two, similar meanings. In portfolio theory, dominance is a characteristic of portfolios on the efficient frontier (EF). Portfolios on the EF are said to dominate any portfolio below the efficient frontier. In a similar fashion, during the editing phase of prospect theory, an investor will eliminate any investment opportunity he perceives as being dominated by others.

2. **C** Adding choice C to both A and B will not affect the preference ranking of A and B. If the investor prefers A to B and we add C to both choices, the investor will prefer (A + C) over (B + C). This also applies to adding a portion of C.

3. **A** A rational investor will maximize return for a given level of risk and minimize risk for a given level of return. Rational investors experience decreasing marginal utility, meaning that their utility functions are concave. Each additional unit of wealth increases their utility but at a decreasing rate. Risk-neutral investors more or less ignore risk and have linear utility functions (constant marginal utility), and risk seekers have convex utility functions. We are told the investor is rational, so we can rule out the linear and convex utility functions.

4. **C** An investor who actively seeks risk in investments would be classified as risk seeking and would experience increasing marginal utility; each additional unit of wealth produces more utility than the previous unit, so the investor derives utility out of riskier investments with high expected returns. This investor would have a convex utility function. Constant marginal utility refers to risk-neutral investors with linear utility functions, and decreasing marginal utility applies to risk-averse investors with concave utility functions.

5. **B** One of the foundations of prospect theory loss aversion. Investors focus on risk relative to gains and losses (changes in wealth) rather than risk relative to returns. The result is that the disutility associated with a loss is greater than the increase in utility from a gain of the same magnitude.

6.   Determine the investor's subjective probability for each outcome and then find the subjective weighted average utility:

1	2	3	4	
Outcome	Utility	Probability of Occurrence	Subjective Probability Factor, w	Subjective Probability (3 × 4)
–8%	–120	15%	1.25	18.75%
0%	–10	40%	1.15	46.00%
6%	50	30%	0.85	25.50%
10%	100	15%	0.65	9.75%
Total	20	100%		

$$\text{Exp(Utility)} = wP_{-8\%}U_{-8\%} + wP_{0\%}U_{0\%} + wP_{6\%}U_{6\%} + wP_{10\%}U_{10\%}$$
$$= 0.1875(-120) + 0.46(-10) + 0.255(50) + 0.0975(100)$$
$$= -22.50 - 4.6 + 12.75 + 9.75 = -4.60$$

The investor is **not likely** to make the investment because its subjective probability-weighted average utility is negative.

7.   The manager's actions are indicative of *bounded rationality*. According to bounded rationality, investors attempt to make the most rational decision possible based on an amount of information they deem satisfactory. Rather than gather and analyze all relevant available information, the investor gathers and analyzes enough information to make a positive decision, not necessarily the optimal decision. Note that *satisficing* would have been an acceptable answer with the same discussion.

8. **A**   Satisficing refers to making the most rational decision possible given the available information and the investor's limited cognitive ability. Rather than making the optimal, utility-maximizing decision, investors act as rationally as possible in making decisions (bounded rationality). Each decision is seen as suboptimal but positive in that it moves the investor toward the desired goal.

9.

Statement	Agree/Disagree	Justification
"I don't care who you are. If the stock market is semi-strong efficient, no information can consistently generate excess returns. There are no free lunches!"	Disagree	Semi-strong efficiency only deals with public information. Non-public information can still generate excess return.
"The January effect supports the assertion that markets are not strong-form efficient."	Agree	The January effect is a calendar anomaly suggesting simple public price data can be used to add value. This violates all three forms of the EMH.

Non-public information could include proprietary analysis methods, advance knowledge of supply and demand, and material non-public information. Of course, some of this information would be unethical to act on. The simple statement semi-strong efficiency precludes excess return is false because it ignores the issue of non-public information. This question tests whether you understand that there are three versions of the efficient market hypothesis.

10. **B**   Support levels act like floors to security or index price levels. As the security or index price approaches the floor, buy pressure tends to push it up. Resistance levels act like ceilings. As the security or index price approaches the resistance level, sell pressure tends to push it down.

11. **A**   The numbers 11,000 and 10,000 represent a technical trading band formed by a resistance level (11,000) and a support level (10,000). Support and resistance levels are technical trading indicators and are usually considered evidence against weak-form efficiency.

12.   An underlying assumption of the efficient markets hypothesis is that arbitrage forces will move instantaneously to correct mispricing. Liquidity concerns, however, can delay or even prohibit the forces of arbitrage. For example, a hedge fund manager may be constrained from quickly taking a position because of liquidity constraints. If the fund is open quarterly for subscription or withdrawal, liquidity needs are uncertain. Realizing he may have to meet liquidity needs by unwinding a position before the profit is realized or even at a loss, the manager can be hesitant to assume the position in the first place. If enough managers face similar constraints, market prices could stray from their intrinsic values and remain that way for extended periods.

13.

Statement	Agree/Disagree	Justification
"The behavioral asset pricing model incorporates a sentiment premium when valuing assets. For example, the more strongly analysts feel about a security, the greater the sentiment premium and the higher the price."	Disagree	The sentiment premium in the BAPM can be derived from the agreement or disagreement among analysts, not the strengths of their sentiments per se. The more widely dispersed analysts' opinions, the greater the sentiment premium, the higher the discount rate applied to assets' cash flows, and the lower their prices.

THE BEHAVIORAL BIASES OF INDIVIDUALS[1]

EXAM FOCUS

This assignment builds on the previous reading. It goes into more details on various biases. Expect exam questions that present situations where you must identify which bias or biases are displayed. Because many of the biases are closely related, read each exam situation closely and identify from the facts presented which bias is the best fit to the facts. Also know the implications of a bias on investment decision making or policy and be able to identify whether it is better to accommodate or mitigate a bias.

COGNITIVE ERRORS AND EMOTIONAL BIASES

The assumptions of traditional finance that individuals act as rational economic men who objectively consider all relevant information to make rational decisions and that this process results in efficient markets is not completely accurate. Behavioral finance looks at normal behavior of individual market participants (Behavioral Finance Micro) and the effect of such behavior on markets (Behavioral Finance Macro). A better understanding of the biases of clients (and of the professionals who work with those clients) should allow for the construction of portfolios that better approximate the efficiency of traditional finance and with which clients are better able to adhere to with during adverse conditions.

LOS 6.a: Distinguish between cognitive errors and emotional biases.

Cognitive errors are due primarily to faulty reasoning and could arise from a lack of understanding proper statistical analysis techniques, information processing mistakes, faulty reasoning, or memory errors. Such errors can often be corrected or mitigated with better training or information. In contrast emotional biases are not related to conscious thought and stem from feelings or impulses or intuition. As such they are more difficult to overcome and may have to be accommodated. Despite the distinction in grouping biases as either cognitive or emotional, a bias may have elements of both cognition and emotion. When trying to overcome or mitigate biases that are both emotional and cognitive, success is more likely by focusing on the cognitive issues.

---

1. Terminology used throughout this topic review is industry convention as presented in Reading 6 of the 2017 CFA Level III exam curriculum.

©2016 Kaplan, Inc.

Professor's Note: You should always look at the combination of facts and information presented in any question to see if the bias in a particular situation is arising more from cognitive or emotional thinking before determining if it is likely it can be mitigated or if it must be accommodated.

LOS 6.b: Discuss commonly recognized behavioral biases and their implications for financial decision making.

LOS 6.c: Identify and evaluate an individual's behavioral biases.

LOS 6.d: Evaluate how behavioral biases affect investment policy and asset allocation decisions and recommend approaches to mitigate their effects.

Cognitive Errors

While cognitive errors arise primarily from statistical or information or reasoning deficiencies or faulty memory, they can also have an emotional element. Market participants may unconsciously tilt away from behavior that causes personal distress or pain while tilting towards behavior that causes pleasure. In general cognitive errors are easier to mitigate or correct with better information, asking the right questions, or seeking qualified advice.

Cognitive errors can be divided into 5 "belief perseverance" biases that reflect a desire to stick with a previous decision and 4 "processing errors" where the information analysis process is flawed.

Professor's Note: Candidates regularly complain that many BF terms mean the same thing. (1) This is partially true and exam questions will be written so there is a best answer choice. (2) The main terms are not the same. Keep definitions short and the differences become more apparent.

Candidates also complain that there are too many terms. The solution is to show judgment and focus on the terms that are discussed in detail and/or multiple times.

In the following section, a useful short distinguishing characteristic of main terms is in bold.

Cognitive Errors: Belief Perseverance

1. **Conservatism bias** occurs when market participants **rationally form an initial view but then fail to change that view as new information becomes available**. In Bayesian terminology they overweight the initial probabilities and do not adjust probabilities for the new information.

> **Example: Conservatism**
>
> John Mue has carefully analyzed the historical data and concluded that recessionary environments occur on average 20% of the time. Mue has incorporated this probability into his strategic asset allocation recommendations. When new information is presented by a coworker showing that the actions of the central bank significantly affect the recession probabilities and that the new head of the central bank has announced tightening monetary conditions, Mue goes on vacation without making any adjustments to his work.
>
> **Answer:**
>
> Mue is showing conservatism by sticking with his original work and not considering the impact of the new information. In this case there may be an emotional aspect as well as Mue chooses the pleasure of a vacation over doing hard work.

Consequences and implications of conservatism may include market participants who are:

- Unwilling or slow to update a view and therefore hold an investment too long.
- Hold an investment too long to avoid the mental effort or stress of updating a view.

Conservatism detection starts with participants becoming aware of their own biases. The more difficult the thought process or information, the more likely conservatism bias will occur. Conversely easy changes may be made too often because they involve little mental effort. Thus conservatism can lead to either too little or too much change and turnover.

2. **Confirmation bias** occurs when market participants **look for new information or distort new information to support an existing view**. It is a kind of selection bias. Client's who get involved with the portfolio process by researching some of their portfolio holdings may become overly attached to some holdings and only bring up information favorable to the holding. This would be confirmation bias.

Consequences and implications of confirmation may include market participants who:

- Consider positive but ignore negative information and therefore hold investments too long.
- Set up the decision process or data screens incorrectly to find what they want to see.
- Under diversify as they become overly convinced their ideas are correct.
- Over concentrate in the stock of their employer believing they have an information advantage in to that security.

Confirmation detection starts with seeking out contrary views and information. For example if an analyst focuses on bottom up fundamental financial statement analysis then the analyst could consult with a top down economic forecaster to gain an alternative view.

3. **Representativeness** is based on a belief **the past will persist and new information is classified based on past experience or classification.** While this may be efficient, the new information can be misunderstood if is classified based on a superficial resemblance to the past or a classification. Two forms of representativeness include:

   - **Base rate neglect**, where the base rate (probability) of the initial classification is not adequately considered. Essentially the classification is taken as being 100% correct with no consideration that it could be wrong. A stock could be classified as a value stock and new information about the stock analyzed based on that classification. In reality, it may not be a value stock.
   - **Sample-size neglect** makes the initial classification based on an overly small and potentially unrealistic sample of data. For example, the initial classification of the stock could be based on dividend yield without considering any of the other typical characteristics of a value stock.

Example: Representativeness

XYZ company has long been recognized as a growth stock delivering superior earnings growth and stock price appreciation. While earnings have continued to grow, last year's revenue has not and neither has the stock price. If an analyst suffers from base-rate neglect and sample-size neglect would he be more likely to buy or sell the stock? What if the analyst treats the growth classification as representative?

Answer:

If the analyst exhibits sample-size and base-rate neglect the analyst will ignore XYZ's long record as a growth stock, focus on the short-term disappointing result and may recommend sale without considering the long term possibility it will revert to growth behavior.

However if the analyst over relies on the initial growth classification the analyst may assume it will return to growth and recommend purchase without properly considering all of the recent results.

Consequences and implications of representativeness may include market participants who:

- Attach too much importance to new pieces of information and have excessive turnover.
- Make decisions based on simple rules of thumb and classification without thorough and more difficult analysis, attaching either too much or too little importance to new information.

Representativeness detection starts with a better understanding of the laws of probability and statistical analysis. Helpful questions that might detect the bias include assessing the probability a given investment is properly categorized in a certain group of ideas and not in a different group. By thinking in probabilities, it is more likely risk will be considered and sufficient diversification will occur.

In evaluating the performance of a portfolio this would include analyzing: How the performance compares to similar portfolios (rather than to the general market alone)? Have there been changes in the managers of the portfolio? What is the general reputation of the manager? Has the portfolio or manager changed style or investment approach due to changing conditions?

4. **Illusion of control bias** exists when **market participants think they can control or affect outcomes when they cannot.** It is often associated with emotional biases: *illusion of knowledge* (belief you know things you do not know), *self-attribution* (belief you personally caused something to happen), and *overconfidence biases* (an unwarranted belief you are correct).

   Consequences and implications of illusion of control may include market participants who:

   - Trade more than is appropriate as they mistakenly believe they can control the outcome of a trade or are overconfident in their analysis.
   - Fail to adequately diversify.

   Illusion of control detection starts with realizing investment results are probabilistic. Participants should seek out opposing viewpoints to consider alternative outcomes. Keeping good records to document the thinking behind ideas and reviewing results to see if there are patterns behind which ideas work, which don't, and the actual past probability of being right is essential.

5. **Hindsight bias** is a **selective memory of past events, actions, or what was knowable in the past.** Participants tend to remember their correct views and forget the errors. They also overestimate what could have been known.

   Consequences and implications of hindsight may include market participants who:

   - Overestimate the rate at which they correctly predicted events which could reinforce an emotional overconfidence bias.
   - Become overly critical of the performance of others. For example they might criticize the stock selections of an analyst whose recommendations underperformed the market when the recommendations outperformed the market groups for which the analyst was responsible.

   Hindsight detection starts with asking questions like "Do I really remember what I predicted and recommended?" Participants should also maintain and review complete records to determine past errors as well as successes. They should remember there will be periods when strategies are in or out of favor and review success relative to appropriate benchmarks.

Cognitive Errors: Information-Processing Biases

These are related more to the processing of information and less to the decision making process.

1. **Anchoring and adjustment bias** occurs when market participants use psychological heuristic experience based trial and error rules to unduly affect probabilities. **Changes are made but in relation to the initial view and therefore the changes are inadequate.** Generally when individuals are forced to estimate an unknown, they often select an arbitrary initial value and then try to adjust it up or down as they process information. This makes it closely related to conservatism and a reluctance to change as new information is received. New information is not dependent on initial estimates or starting points and the new data should be objectively considered without regard to any initial anchor point.

   Consequences and implications of anchoring and adjustment may include market participants who stay anchored to an initial estimate and do not adjust for new information.

   Anchoring and adjustment detection starts with asking questions such as "Am I staying with this stock because I originally recommended it at a higher price. In other words am I becoming dependent on that previous price? Or would I recommend it based on an all new analysis if this was the first time I evaluated it?"

2. **Mental accounting bias** arises when **money is treated differently depending on how it is categorized.** For example a client might mentally treat wages differently from a bonus when determining saving and investment goals.

   Consequences and implications of mental accounting may include market participants:

   - Structuring portfolios in layers to meet different priority goals. This may help clients overcome other biases. But it ignores correlation between layers of the portfolio and results can be suboptimal from a traditional perspective.
   - Failing to lower portfolio risk by adding assets with very low correlation.
   - Segregating return into arbitrary categories of income, realized gains and losses, or unrealized gains and losses. The result tends to be an overemphasis on income generating assets, resulting in a lower total return.

   Mental accounting could be detected by examining what the portfolio could have achieved if the entire client assets were examined as one portfolio considering the effects of correlation among all parts of the portfolio. An excessive focus on source of return (i.e., income versus price appreciation) could be detected by analyzing the maximum total return consistent with the investor's risk objective and constraints. If this is considerably better than the existing expected return of the portfolio, too much attention is being placed on source of return. For example, if the portfolio has an expected return of 6.7% and the return is primarily income but another portfolio with the same risk but less income has an expected return of 7.5%, it would appear better to accept the portfolio generating less income.

Professor's Note: It is important not to jump to simplistic labeling of something as all good or all bad. For example layering a portfolio can be a "good" way help a client untrained in the concepts of portfolio theory to make better decisions yet it can be "bad" in not achieving a fully optimal portfolio.

3. **Framing bias** occurs **when decisions are affected by the way in which the question or data is "framed."** In other words, the way the question is framed affects how the information is processed leading to the answer given. For instance, if a stock is priced at GBP20 and that is compared to a cost basis of GBP 15, the holder is more likely to sell (and experience the pleasure of realizing a gain). But if the price of GBP20 is compared to a previous close of GBP25, the holder is less likely to sell (and experience the pain of a loss). If only one or two reference points are considered (as above), it could be called *narrow framing*.

> **Example: Decision framing bias**
>
> Investors were shown 3 efficient portfolios and the 95% confidence interval of expected returns for each portfolio. For example the first portfolio was shown as having a range of 0.1% to 6.7%, while the other portfolios had wider ranges. Next the same portfolios were shown but the expected return was listed and then the standard deviation. If investors show loss aversion and framing bias, under which conditions would the investors be likely to pick the lowest return portfolio?
>
> **Answer:**
>
> If shown the range of returns they would be more likely to pick the lowest returning portfolio because it frames the data to show the first portfolio with a positive lower return while the other portfolios, with wider ranges, are more likely to show a lower number that is negative. The first number seen in the display of data is framing the final decision. In contrast the other display of data starts with expected positive return numbers and does not directly show any negative numbers, only a standard deviation. Thus investors often select a portfolio with a higher return number.
>
> A number of other biases might also be present. Because the example distinguishes how the information is displayed, and the order the information is presented, decision framing is the best answer.

Consequences and implications of framing bias may include market participants who:

- Fail to properly assess risk and end up overly risk-averse or risk-seeking.
- Choose suboptimal risk for their portfolio or assets based on the way a presentation is made.
- Become overly concerned with short term price movement and trade too often.

Framing could be detected by asking a question such as "Is my decision based on realizing a gain or a loss?" Instead a more appropriate analysis might compare current price to intrinsic value analysis.

4. **Availability bias** starts with putting **undue emphasis on the information that is readily available.** It is a mental short cut to focus excessively on what is easy to get. It can include some or all of the following:

    - Retrievability, which is simply to focus on what is first thought of.
    - Categorization, which puts excessive emphasis on how an idea is first categorized. For instance a manager assumes a stock is a growth stock and therefore screens it for issues such as P/E and growth rate (failing to consider other issues like leverage ratios).
    - Narrow range of experience could occur when the frame of reference is too narrow. For example a CFA Level III candidate prepares for the exam by working all of the old exam questions. The candidate then says it is unfair when other types of questions are asked on the exam. The frame of reference is too narrow, especially when the readings change and old questions and answers may no longer be relevant.
    - Resonance occurs when individuals assume what interests them is representative of what other people will find important.

    Consequences and implications of availability may include market participants who:

    - Choose a manager based on advertizing or recalling they have heard the name.
    - Limit investment choices to what they are familiar with resulting in:
        - Under diversification.
        - Inappropriate asset allocation.

    Availability could be overcome by maintaining a carefully researched and constructed Investment Policy Statement (IPS); through appropriate research and analysis of all decisions; and a long term focus. Questions such as "where did I hear of this idea could help detect availability bias." Problems created by availability include overreacting and trading too much based on recent and easily available news or relying on available information or opinions that are of low quality and relevance.

Emotional Biases

While there is no formally accepted definition, these six biases generally arise from emotion and feelings rather than any conscious thought.

Professor's Note: Some of the terms about to be discussed here have already come up in the discussion of cognitive biases. If the context of a discussion emphasizes a view is based on unconscious emotion that the holder is unwilling or unable to change it will be more appropriate to see it as an emotional bias. On the other hand if the facts suggest the bias can be overcome with a relatively simple change in thought process or information it is better to see it as a cognitive bias.

1. **Loss-aversion bias** has already been well discussed previously. It arises from **feeling more pain from a loss than pleasure from an equal gain.**

    Consequences and implications of loss-aversion may include:

    - Feeling less pleasure in a gain in value for a profit than pain in a decline in value for an equal loss.

- To avoid the pain of loss an investment holder will tend to hold on to losers too long but may sell winners too quickly.
- Trade too much by selling for small gains which raises transaction costs and lowers returns.
- Incurring too much risk by continuing to hold assets that have deteriorated in quality and lost value.
- If an initial decline in value occurs, then taking excessive risk in the hope of recovering. Investment managers can be particularly susceptible to this behavior.
- Allowing the framing of the reference point to determine if a position is seen as a gain or loss.
- Treating money that is made on a trade differently than other funds and taking excess risk with such money.
- **Myopic loss aversion occurs when the shorter term risk of stocks incorrectly leads to an excessively high equity risk premiums in the market.** The excessive risk premium ignores that long-term equity returns are favorable and leads to general underpricing and under-weighting of equity in portfolios.

Loss aversion could be overcome by maintaining a disciplined well thought out process based on future prospects of an investment, not perceived gain or loss.

2. **Overconfidence bias** occurs when **market participants overestimate their own intuitive ability or reasoning**. It can show up as *illusion of knowledge* where they think they do a better job of predicting than they actually do. Combined with *self-attribution bias*, individuals will take personal credit when things go right (*self-enhancing*) but blame others or circumstances for failure (*self-protecting*). While it is both cognitive and emotional, it is more emotional in nature because it is difficult for most individuals to correct and is rooted in the desire to feel good.

Overconfidence arising from an illusion of knowledge is based a general feeling that the individual will be right. *Prediction overconfidence* leads individuals to underestimate uncertainty and standard deviation of their predictions while *certainty overconfidence* occurs when they overstate the probability they will be right.

Consequences and implications of overconfidence may include:

- Underestimate risk and overestimate return.
- Under diversification.
- Excessive turnover and transaction costs resulting in lower return.

Overconfidence might be overcome by establishing long-term financial goals with a budget to assure adequate savings and investments are made to meet all goals. In other words, maintain an Investment Policy Statement and Strategic Asset Allocation.

3. **Self-control bias** occurs when **individuals lack self-discipline and favor immediate gratification over long-term goals**.

> **Self-Control Failure**
>
> Many CFA candidates fail the Level III exam the first time because they do not exercise sufficient self-control to study enough.
>
> However it is combining a failure of self-control with other biases that causes the more serious problems:
>
> *   Overconfidence due to assuming that passing Levels I and II will indicate success at Level III.
> *   Representativeness as they assume the way they studied and the exam skills required at Levels I and II will be sufficient at Level III.

Consequences and implications of self-control may include:

*   Insufficient savings accumulation to fund retirement needs.
*   Taking excessive risk in the portfolio to try and compensate for insufficient savings accumulation.
*   An overemphasis on income producing assets to meet shorter term distribution needs.

 Professor's Note: You should be noticing a number of references to the idea analyzing a portfolio on a total return basis and not income versus change in value. This theme will continue in later sessions. Total return is the general approach to take on the exam unless given specific direction otherwise.

Self-control bias might be overcome by establishing an appropriate investment plan and a budget to achieve sufficient savings. Both should be reviewed on a regular basis.

4. **Status quo bias** occurs when **comfort with the existing situation leads to an unwillingness to make changes.** If investment choices include the option to maintain existing choices, or if a choice will happen unless the participant opts out; status quo choices become more likely.

Consequences and implications of status quo may include:

*   Holding portfolios with inappropriate risk.
*   Not considering other, better investment options.

Status quo is very hard to overcome so education regarding reasonable risk/return combinations and the danger of overconcentration in an (employer's) stock is essential.

Professor's Note: Status quo and the next two biases are very closely related. But status quo is maintaining a choice out of inertia, while endowment bias arises when some intangible value unrelated to investment merit is assigned to a holding, and regret-aversion is just what it says, if you make a change and it goes badly you will feel bad about it so do nothing and then you are not to blame. All three can lead to the same result (keep what you have) but the reason for doing so is slightly different.

5. **Endowment bias** occurs when **an asset is felt to be special and more valuable simply because it is already owned.** For example, when one spouse holds on to the securities their deceased spouse purchased for some reason like sentiment that is unrelated to the current merits of the securities. In studies individuals have been asked to state their minimum sale price for an asset they own (say $25) and their maximum purchase price (say $23). The fact that they will sell it at a price higher than they would pay has been explained as endowment. Once they own it, they act as if it is worth more than they would pay.

Consequences and implications of endowment may include:

- Failing to sell an inappropriate asset resulting in inappropriate asset allocation.
- Holding things you are familiar with because they provide some intangible sense of comfort.

Endowment is common with inherited assets and might be detected or mitigated by asking a question such as "Would you make this same investment with new money today?" If inherited assets are significant holdings in the portfolio it may be essential to address the bias. Starting a disciplined diversification program could be a way to ease the discomfort of sales.

6. **Regret-aversion bias** occurs when market participants **do nothing out of excess fear that actions could be wrong.** They attach undue weight to actions of commission (doing something) and don't consider actions of omission (doing nothing). Their sense of regret and pain is stronger for acts of commission.

Consequences and implications of regret-aversion may include:

- Excess conservatism in the portfolio because it is easy to see that riskier assets do at times underperform. Therefore, do not buy riskier assets and you won't experience regret when they decline.
- This leads to long-term underperformance and a failure to meet goals.
- *Herding behavior* is a form of regret-aversion where participants go with the consensus or popular opinion. Essentially the participants tell themselves they are not to blame if others are wrong too.

Regret-aversion might be mitigated through effective communication on the benefits of diversification, the outcomes consistent with the efficient frontier tradeoff of risk/return, and the consequences of not meeting critical long-term investment goals.

Further Implications of Biases on Investment Policy and Asset Allocation

Investment practitioners who understand behavioral biases have a better chance of constructing and managing portfolios that benefit normal clients. By first acknowledging and then accommodating or modifying biases, more optimal results are likely. This starts with asking the right questions:

- What are the biases of the client?
- Are they primarily emotional or cognitive?
- How do they effect portfolio asset allocation?
- Should the biases be moderated or adapted to?
- Is a behaviorally modified asset allocation warranted?
- What are the appropriate quantifiable modifications?

Goals-Based Investing (GBI)

 Professor's Note: GBI will be similar to the layers in behavioral portfolio theory (BPT). BPT explained the layers as reflecting whether higher return or lower risk was important to the goal. GBI starts with the importance of achieving the goal.

GBI starts with establishing the relative importance to the client of each of the client's goals.

- Essential needs and obligations should be identified and quantified first. These would include essential living expenses and should be met with low risk investments as the base layer of the portfolio assets.
- Next might come desired outcomes such as annual giving to charity which can be met with a layer of moderate risk investments.
- Finally low priority aspirations such as increasing the value of the portfolio to leave it to a foundation at death could be met with higher risk investments.

GBI is consistent with the concept of loss-aversion in prospect theory. The client can see that more important goals are exposed to less risky assets and less potential loss. It is better suited to wealth preservation than to wealth accumulation. By utilizing the mental accounting of layers to meet goals, the client can better understand the construction of the portfolio.

Behaviorally Modified Asset Allocation (BMAA)

BMAA is another approach to asset allocation that incorporates the client's behavioral biases. A worst case scenario for many clients is to abandon an investment strategy during adverse periods. The outcome can be very detrimental because the change is likely to occur at a low point, right before a recovery for the strategy begins. Determining in advance a strategy the client can adhere to during adverse periods would be a better outcome. BMAA considers whether it is better to moderate or adapt to the client's biases in order to construct a portfolio the client can stick with.

BMAA starts with identifying an optimal strategic asset allocation consistent with traditional finance. It then considers the relative wealth of the client and the emotional versus cognitive nature of the client's biases to adjust that allocation.

- A high level of wealth versus lifestyle and what the client considers essential needs would be a low standard of living risk (SLR). With a low SLR the client can afford to deviate from an optimal portfolio. The rich can afford to be eccentric.
- Biases that are primarily cognitive in nature are easier to modify. Working with the client can accomplish this and allow for less deviation from a traditionally efficient portfolio mix.
- In contrast emotionally based biases are generally harder to modify and may have to be accommodated, resulting in a less efficient portfolio.
- Finally the amount of deviation to accept from a traditional optimal allocation should be established. Typically this would be done by setting a range in which an asset class can deviate from optimal before it must be adjusted back. For example suppose an optimal allocation would call for 60% equity for the client.

The table below demonstrates how the process could be implemented in order to create an asset allocation that the client will be able to adhere to over the long run.

Figure 1: When to Accommodate Versus When to Modify

Relative Wealth (RW) and SLR:	Biases are Primarily:	Accommodate to or Modify the Biases of the Client:	Allowable Deviations Up or Down from Optimal Weight:
High RW and low SLR	Emotional	Accommodate	10 to 15%
High RW and low SLR	Cognitive	Some of both	5 to 10%
Low RW and high SLR	Emotional	Some of both	5 to 10%
Low RW and high SLR	Cognitive	Modify	0 to 3%

- The specific deviation numbers chosen are arbitrary and are intended to show that low SLR and emotional biases can be accommodated with large deviations from the optimal weights. The client can afford to allow their emotions to be accommodated.
- In contrast high SLR and cognitive errors require the biases be addressed with the client and moderated to achieve a near optimal asset allocation. Those with low wealth cannot afford to deviate and cognitive errors are easier to overcome.
- The other two cases fall in between.

Case Study, Ms. Z:

Ms. Z is a new client of BF Advisors. BF begins each client relationship with an extensive set of interviews. These interviews determined Ms. Z has very low needs in relation to her wealth. With even modest diversification there is no reasonable likelihood she could outlive her assets. In addition she is expected to inherit large sums from her mother's estate. The estate settlement is expected in the next year.

BF also uses a set of standardized questions to identify the biases of each client. Ms. Z shows strong tendencies to conservatism, sample-size neglect, framing, endowment, and availability biases. After completing the questions she meets with her BF portfolio manager and asks for further information regarding the biases. She has always enjoyed studying new areas and learning new approaches to life.

Recommend whether her biases should be accommodated or modified, and whether her portfolio will deviate from a traditional optimal allocation.

Answer:

Ms. Z has very low SLR which would allow her biases to be accommodated however her biases are primarily cognitive (except for endowment bias). In addition she likes to learn suggesting that it may be easy to moderate her biases. Therefore a mix of accommodation and modification is appropriate, though in her case we will lean towards modification and smaller deviations from a traditional optimal asset allocation.

KEY CONCEPTS

LOS 6.a

Cognitive errors result from the inability to analyze information or from basing decisions on partial information. Individuals try to process information into rational decisions, but they lack the capacity or sufficient information to do so. Cognitive errors can be divided into belief perseverance errors and processing errors. **Emotional biases** are caused by the way individuals frame the information and the decision rather than the mechanical or physical process used to analyze and interpret it. Emotional bias is more of a spontaneous reaction.

LOS 6.b,c

Cognitive Errors: Belief Perseverance
- Conservatism bias.
- Confirmation bias.
- Representativeness bias.
- Control bias.
- Hindsight bias.

Cognitive Errors: Information Processing
- Anchoring and adjustment.
- Mental accounting bias.
- Framing bias.
- Availability bias.

Emotional Biases
- Loss aversion bias.
- Overconfidence bias.
- Self-control bias.
- Status quo bias.
- Endowment bias.
- Regret-aversion bias.

LOS 6.d

Conservatism Bias
Impact: Slow to react to new information or avoid the difficulties associated with analyzing new information. Can also be explained in terms of Bayesian statistics; place too much weight on the base rates.
Mitigation: Look carefully at the new information itself to determine its value.

Confirmation Bias
Impact: Focus on positive information about an investment and ignore or dismiss anything negative. Can lead to too much confidence in the investment and to overweighting it in the portfolio.
Mitigation: Actively seek out information that seems to contradict your opinions and analyze it carefully.

Representativeness Bias

Impact: Place information into categories utilizing an if-then heuristic. Place too much emphasis on perceived category of new information. Likely to change strategies based on a small sample of information.

Mitigation: Consciously take steps to avoid base rate neglect and sample size neglect. Consider the true probability that information fits a category. Use *Periodic Table of Investment Returns.*

Illusion of Control Bias

Impact: The illusion of control over one's investment outcomes can lead to excessive trading with the accompanying costs. Can also lead to concentrated portfolios.

Mitigation: Seek opinions of others. Keep records of trades to see if successful at controlling investment outcomes.

Hindsight Bias

Impact: Overestimate accuracy of their forecasts and take too much risk.

Mitigation: Keep detailed record of all forecasts, including the data analyzed and the reasoning behind the forecast.

Anchoring and Adjustment

Impact: Tend to remain focused on and stay close to their original forecasts or interpretations.

Mitigation: Give new information thorough consideration to determine its impact on the original forecast or opinion.

Mental Accounting Bias

Impact: Portfolios tend to resemble layered pyramids of assets. Subconsciously ignore the correlations of assets. May consider income and capital gains separately rather than as parts of the same total return.

Mitigation: Look at all investments as if they are part of the same portfolio to analyze their correlations and determine true portfolio allocation.

Framing Bias

Impact: Narrow a frame of reference; individuals focus on one piece or category of information and lose sight of the overall situation or how the information fits into the overall scheme of things.

Mitigation: Investors should focus on expected returns and risk, rather than on gains or losses. That includes assets or portfolios with existing gains or losses.

Availability Bias: Four causes are retrievability, categorization, narrow range of experience, and resonance.

Impact: Select investments based on how easily their memories are retrieved and categorized. Narrow range of experience can lead to concentrated portfolios.

Mitigation: Develop an IPS and construct a suitable portfolio through diligent research.

Loss Aversion Bias

Myopic loss aversion combines the effects of time horizon and framing.

Impact: Focus on current gains and losses. Continue to hold losers in hopes of breaking even. Sell winners to capture the gains.

Mitigation: Perform a thorough fundamental analysis. Overcome mental anguish of recognizing losses.

Overconfidence Bias

Impact: Hold under-diversified portfolios; underestimate the downside while overestimating the upside potential. Trade excessively.

Mitigation: Keep detailed records of trades, including the motivation for each trade. Analyze successes and losses relative to the strategy used.

Self-Control Bias

Impact: Lack discipline to balance short-term gratification with long-term goals. Tend to try to make up the shortfall by assuming too much risk.

Mitigation: Maintain complete, clearly defined investment goals and strategies. Budgets help deter the propensity to over-consume.

Status Quo Bias

Impact: Risk characteristics of the portfolio change. Investor loses out on potentially profitable assets.

Mitigation: Education about risk and return and proper asset. Difficult to mitigate.

Endowment Bias

Impact: Value of owned assets higher than same assets if not owned. Stick with assets because of familiarity and comfort or were inherited.

Mitigation: Determine whether the asset allocation is appropriate.

Regret Aversion Bias

Impact: Stay in low-risk investments. Portfolio with limited upside potential. Stay in familiar investments or "follow the herd."

Mitigation: Education is primary mitigation tool.

Goals-based investing recognizes that individuals are subject to loss aversion and mental accounting. Builds a portfolio in layers, each consisting of assets used to meet individual goals. Pyramiding: bottom layer comprised of assets designated to meet the investor's most important goals. Each successive layer consists of increasingly risky assets used to meet less and less import goals. Provides investor with ability to see risk more clearly. Although portfolio probably won't be efficient, it will tend to be fairly well diversified.

Behaviorally Modified Asset Allocation

- Emotional biases are more often accommodated through deviations from the rational asset portfolio allocation.
- Higher wealth relative to lifestyle needs allows for greater deviations from the rational portfolio.
- The emotional biases of the lower-wealth individual are treated about the same as the cognitive biases of the wealthier individual.
- The amount of deviation is also affected by the number of different asset classes in the portfolio.
- The lower the suggested deviation from the rational portfolio asset allocation, the greater the need to mitigate the investor's behavioral biases.
  - Due to significant standard of living risk, for example, the cognitive biases of the low-wealth investor must be mitigated.

CONCEPT CHECKERS

1. Which of the following would *most likely* be classified as an emotional bias? The investor:
   A. has difficulty interpreting complex new information.
   B. only partially adjusts forecasts when he receives new information.
   C. has a tendency to value the same assets higher if he owns them than if he does not own them.

2. Which of the following would *most likely* indicate that an investor is subject to an emotional bias?
   A. Regularly basing decisions on only a subset of available information.
   B. Reacting spontaneously to a negative earnings announcement by quickly selling a stock.
   C. Remaining invested in a profitable technology stock even though new information indicates its PE ratio is too high.

3. A cognitive error is *best* indicated by which of the following?
   A. Taking more and more risk because the investor mentally attributes his recent investing success to his strategies.
   B. Ending up with a suboptimal asset allocation because the investor does not use a holistic approach to construct the portfolio.
   C. Experiencing a significant loss on an investment because the investor hoped to recover from a negative position that subsequently worsened.

4. Don Henry has just received new information regarding his investment in Orange, Inc. The new information appears to conflict with his earlier forecast of what the stock price should be at this point. Nonetheless, he is unwilling to incorporate the new information into his forecast and to revise it accordingly. What behavioral trait is Henry displaying?
   A. Conservatism bias.
   B. Confirmation bias.
   C. Anchoring and adjustment.

5. Abby Lane is a savvy investor who has investments scattered across many different accounts, from bank savings and before- and after-tax retirement accounts to taxable nonretirement accounts. She also has several different investing goals ranging from important short-term goals to longer-term "wish list" goals. Even though she has many investments along with different goals, she is smart enough to take into consideration the correlation between her assets. She allocates the assets according to her risk-return profile across different asset classes, viewing the investments as comprising a single portfolio with a single measure of risk. What behavioral trait would represent the *opposite* way Lane approaches investing?
   A. Framing bias.
   B. Mental accounting.
   C. Overconfidence bias.

6. Twenty years ago, Jane Ivy set up her initial asset allocation in her defined contribution plan by placing an equal amount in each asset class and never changed it. Over time, she increased her contribution by 1% per year until she reached the maximum amount allowed by law. Due to her steadfastness and good fortune, coupled with matching funds from her employer, she now finds herself in her early 40s with a million-dollar retirement account. Which of the following biases does Ivy suffer from, and how should she remedy that bias?
    A. Representativeness; make sure the sample size is correct and new information is interpreted correctly.
    B. Status quo bias; educate the investor on tradeoffs between risk and return and subsequent proper asset allocation.
    C. Availability bias; develop an investment policy statement through diligent research rather than information that is readily available.

For more questions related to this topic review, log in to your Schweser online account and launch SchweserPro™ QBank; and for video instruction covering each LOS in this topic review, log in to your Schweser online account and launch the OnDemand video lectures, if you have purchased these products.

ANSWERS – CONCEPT CHECKERS

1. **C**   This describes the *endowment bias*, where individuals place a higher value on assets they own than if they did not own those same assets. The other two answer choices describe cognitive errors that are due to the inability to analyze all the information.

2. **B**   Emotional biases tend to elicit more of a spontaneous reaction than a cognitive error would. Making a decision based only on partial information is indicative of a cognitive error. Ignoring a high PE ratio could be indicative of the conservatism bias, which is reacting slowly to new information or avoiding analyzing new information. It could also indicate the confirmation bias, where the investor focuses on positive information and ignores negative information. Both conservatism and confirmation biases are cognitive errors of belief perseverance.

3. **B**   This describes the cognitive error of *mental accounting* in which the investor ends up with a layered pyramid as her portfolio. The different layers of investments do not take into consideration the correlation between the assets and are viewed in isolation from each other; thus, the asset allocation tends to be suboptimal from a risk-return perspective. Taking more risk as a result of attributing investing success to a particular strategy represents overconfidence which is an emotional bias.

4. **A**   This describes the conservatism bias where individuals mentally place more emphasis on the information they used to form their original forecast than on new information. Anchoring and adjustment is closely related to the conservatism bias but is characterized as individuals being stuck on a particular forecasting number and is not associated with how investors relate new information to old information as the conservatism bias does. The confirmation bias is when individuals notice only information that agrees with their perceptions or beliefs. They look for confirming evidence while discounting or even ignoring evidence that contradicts their beliefs.

5. **B**   Lane is investing based on traditional finance theory, which assumes investors make rational decisions and view their assets in a single portfolio context with an asset allocation that takes into consideration the correlation between the assets. The *opposite* approach would be *mental accounting*, where the investor views his assets in different "accounts," each with a separate purpose to achieve a separate goal. The resulting portfolio resembles a pyramid comprised of layers with each layer making up a different set of assets used to accomplish a separate goal. The correlation between those assets is not taken into consideration; thus, the assets are usually not optimally allocated among different asset classes. The *framing bias* is when individuals view information differently depending upon how it is received. *Overconfidence* is when people think they know more than they do, have more and better information than others, and are better at interpreting it, leading to under-diversified portfolios and excessive trading.

6. **B**   Ivy is suffering from the *status quo bias*, where investors leave their asset allocation alone and don't change it according to changing market conditions or changes in their own circumstances. The other two answer choices correctly describe ways of mitigating those behavioral traits.

The following is a review of the Behavioral Finance principles designed to address the learning outcome statements set forth by CFA Institute. Cross-Reference to CFA Institute Assigned Reading #7.

BEHAVIORAL FINANCE AND INVESTMENT PROCESSES[1]

Study Session 3

EXAM FOCUS

This topic review focuses on the influence of behavioral traits on all aspects of the investment process—creating the investment policy statement, the client/adviser relationship, portfolio construction, analyst forecasts, and market anomalies. Be able to discuss the benefit to both clients and advisers of incorporating behavioral finance into the client's investment policy statement and the limitations of classifying investors into behavioral types. Be able to explain how behavioral finance influences the client/adviser relationship and to discuss the benefits to both of incorporating the behavioral aspects of investing into the relationship. Understand how investors tend to construct portfolios from a behavioral perspective. Be able to explain how behavioral biases affect analysts in their forecasting and the remedial actions that should be taken to reduce the influence of those biases. Also, know how behavioral biases affect the decision-making processes of investment committees. Lastly, be able to discuss the influence of behavioral biases on entire markets.

CLASSIFYING INVESTORS INTO BEHAVIORAL TYPES

LOS 7.a: Explain the uses and limitations of classifying investors into personality types.

Financial market participants, both investors and financial advisers, have found that when the psychology of investing is recognized in creating the client's investment policy statement and subsequent implementation, the outcome is likely to be favorable. Applying a strictly traditional finance perspective can lead to pitfalls and unpleasant surprises for both the client and adviser. For example, investors who are overly risk averse or risk seeking react more emotionally to investing than would be expected of the typical, average investor. The adviser will have better success by addressing these clients' emotional biases rather than ignoring them and taking a more traditional finance perspective.

The traditional finance perspective seeks to educate clients based on more quantitative measures of investing, such as standard deviation and Sharpe ratios, and these are of little interest to the client who reacts more emotionally to investing. The goal of viewing the client/adviser relationship from a psychological perspective as compared to a purely traditional finance perspective is for the adviser to better understand his client and to

---

1. Terminology used throughout this topic review is industry convention as presented in Reading 7 of the 2017 Level III CFA exam curriculum.

make better investment decisions. By incorporating behavioral biases into clients' IPSs, clients' portfolios will tend to be closer to the efficient frontier, and clients will be more trusting and satisfied and tend to stay on track with their long-term strategic plans. Ultimately, since everyone is happy, the result is a better overall working relationship between client and adviser.

Behavioral Models

We will discuss three behavioral models: (1) the Barnewall two-way model, (2) the Bailard, Biehl, and Kaiser five-way model, and (3) the Pompain model.

The **Barnewall two-way behavioral model**[2] was developed in 1987 and classifies investors into only two types: passive and active. *Passive investors* are those who have not had to risk their own capital to gain wealth. For example they might have gained wealth through long, steady employment and disciplined saving or through inheritance. As a result of accumulating wealth passively, they tend to be more risk averse and have a greater need for security than their "active" counterparts. *Active investors* risk their own capital to gain wealth and usually take an active role in investing their own money. Active investors are much less risk averse than passive investors and are willing to give up security for control over their own wealth creation.

 Professor's Note: The causal relationship between steadily accumulating wealth over time and a high aversion to risk could go in either direction. Either one can lead to the other.

The **Bailard, Biehl, and Kaiser (BB&K) five-way model**[3], developed in 1986, classifies investors along two dimensions according to how they approach life in general. The first dimension, *confidence*, identifies the level of confidence usually displayed when the individual makes decisions. Confidence level can range from confident to anxious. The second dimension, *method of action*, measures the individual's approach to decision making. Depending on whether the individual is methodical in making decisions or tends to be more spontaneous, method of action can range from careful to impetuous.

BB&K categorize investors into five behavioral types, which lie at different points in a grid formed by confidence/method of action. For example, the "straight arrow" investor would lie in the center of the grid, with the other four behavioral types scattered around the center.

Using the two dimensions like axes on a graph, the five behavioral types of the BB&K model are summarized in the following according to confidence and method of action, as indicated in Figure 1.

1. The **adventurer** has the following traits:
    *   Confident and impetuous (northeast quadrant).
    *   Might hold highly concentrated portfolios.

2. Barnewall, Marilyn. 1987. "Psychological Characteristics of the Individual Investor." *Asset Allocation for the Individual Investor*. Charlottesville, VA: The Institute of Chartered Financial Analysts.

3. Bailard, Brad M., David L. Biehl, and Ronald W. Kaiser. 1986. Personal Money Management, 5th ed. Chicago: Science Research Associates.

- Willing to take chances.
- Likes to make own decisions.
- Unwilling to take advice.
- Advisors find them difficult to work with.

2. The **celebrity** has the following traits:
   - Anxious and impetuous (southeast quadrant).
   - Might have opinions but recognizes limitations.
   - Seeks and takes advice about investing.

3. The **individualist** has the following traits:
   - Confident and careful (northwest quadrant).
   - Likes to make own decisions after careful analysis.
   - Good to work with because they listen and process information rationally.

4. The **guardian** has the following traits:
   - Anxious and careful (southwest quadrant).
   - Concerned with the future and protecting assets.
   - May seek the advice of someone they perceive as more knowledgeable than themselves.

5. The **straight arrow** has the following traits:
   - Average investor (intersection of the two dimensions).
   - Neither overly confident nor anxious.
   - Neither overly careful nor impetuous.
   - Willing to take increased risk for increased expected return.

Figure 1: Classification of Investors According to the BB&K Behavioral Model[4]

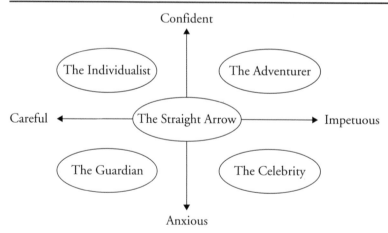

The **Pompian behavioral model**[5], developed in 2008, identifies four behavioral investor types (BITs). Pompian suggests that the adviser go through a 4-step process to determine the investor's BIT.

1. Interview the client to determine if she is active or passive as an indication of her risk tolerance.

---

4. Based on Exhibit 1, 2017 Level III curriculum, vol. 2, p 109.
5. Pompian, Michael. 2008. "Using Behavioral Investor Types to Build Better Relationships with Your Clients." *Journal of Financial Planning*, October 2008: 64-76.

2. Plot the investor on a risk tolerance scale.

3. Test for behavioral biases.

4. Classify the investor into one of the BITs.

Figure 2 shows the results of the Pompian method of classifying investors. You will notice that both the *Passive Preserver* and the *Active Accumulator* tend to make emotional decisions. The *Friendly Follower* and *Independent Individualist* tend to use a more thoughtful approach to decision making. The most common cognitive and emotional biases associated with each investor type are listed following Figure 2.

Figure 2: Four Investor Types, Investment Styles, and Behavioral Biases[6]

Investor Type	*Risk Tolerance*	*Investment Style*	*Decision Making*
Passive Preserver	Low	Conservative	Emotional
Friendly Follower			Cognitive
Independent Individualist	↓	↓	Cognitive
Active Accumulator	High	Aggressive	Emotional

Most common *emotional* biases exhibited:

- **Passive Preserver:** Endowment, loss aversion, status quo, regret aversion.
- **Friendly Follower:** Regret aversion.
- **Independent Individualist:** Overconfidence, self-attribution.
- **Active Accumulator:** Overconfidence, self-control.

Most common *cognitive* biases exhibited:

- **Passive Preserver:** Mental accounting, anchoring and adjustment.
- **Friendly Follower:** Availability, hindsight, framing.
- **Independent Individualist:** Conservatism, availability, confirmation, representativeness.
- **Active Accumulator:** Illusion of control.

Behavioral Investor Types (BITs)

As previously mentioned, the last step in Pompian's process of determining which behavioral bias the investor is exhibiting is to categorize the investor into a behavioral investor type (BIT). There are four BITs, ranging from conservative to aggressive investing. The first BIT is the **Passive Preserver**, characterized as having low risk tolerance, an emotional bias, not willing to risk his own capital, usually not financially sophisticated, and possibly difficult to advise because he is driven by emotion.

---

6. Based on Exhibit 4, 2017 Level III curriculum, vol. 2, p. 113.

The **Friendly Follower** would also be considered a passive investor who has low to moderate risk tolerance and suffers mainly from cognitive errors, which are errors resulting from faulty reasoning and not emotional biases. A Friendly Follower tends to overestimate her risk tolerance and wants to be in the most popular investments with little regard to market conditions or how the investment fits into her overall long-term investment plan. Since a Friendly Follower tends to approach investing from a more cognitive (thinking) perspective, the best course of action in advising her is to use more quantitative methods in educating her on the benefits of portfolio diversification.

The **Independent Individualist** is an active investor who is willing to risk his own capital and give up security to gain wealth. He has moderate to high risk tolerance and suffers from cognitive biases. He is strong-willed, likes to invest, does his own research, and tends to be a contrarian. The Independent Individualist tends to be difficult to advise but will listen to sound advice. Therefore, the best approach to advising him is regular education on investing concepts relevant to the investor.

The **Active Accumulator** is an active investor with a high tolerance for risk who approaches investing from an emotional perspective. The Active Accumulator is an aggressive investor who often comes from an entrepreneurial background and likes to get deeply involved in her investing. She is strong-willed, confident, and likes to control her investing, making her the most difficult of all the BITs to advise. Thus, the best course of action for the adviser is to take control of the investment process and not let the investor control the situation.

Limitations on Classifying Investors into Behavioral Types

Many times, individuals act irrationally at unpredictable moments, making it difficult to apply the different behavioral investor traits consistently for any one investor over a period of time. This leads to several limitations of classifying investors into the various behavioral investor types:

- Many individuals may simultaneously display both emotional biases and cognitive errors. This can make it difficult and inappropriate to try and classify them as to whether their biases are emotional or cognitive; they are both.
- An individual might display traits of more than one behavioral investor type, making it difficult to place the individual into a single category.
- As investors age, they will most likely go through behavioral changes, usually resulting in decreased risk tolerance along with becoming more emotional about their investing.
- Even though two individuals may fall into the same behavioral investor type, the individuals should not necessarily be treated the same due to their unique circumstances and psychological traits.
- Individuals tend to act irrationally at unpredictable times because they are subject to their own specific psychological traits and personal circumstances. In other words, people don't all act irrationally (or rationally) at the same time.

THE CLIENT/ADVISER RELATIONSHIP

LOS 7.b: Discuss how behavioral factors affect adviser–client interactions.

The goal of the client/adviser relationship is constructing a portfolio that the client is comfortable with and will be happy staying in over the long term. This is more easily accomplished once the adviser recognizes the need to incorporate behavior biases into the investment decision-making process.

The success of the typical client/adviser relationship can be measured in four areas, and each one is enhanced by incorporating behavioral finance traits:

1. *The adviser understands the long-term financial goals of the client.* Behavioral finance helps the adviser understand the reasons for the client's goals. The client/adviser relationship is enhanced because the client feels the adviser truly understands him and his needs.

2. *The adviser maintains a consistent approach with the client.* Behavioral finance adds structure and professionalism to the relationship, which helps the adviser understand the client before giving investment advice.

3. *The adviser acts as the client expects.* This is the area that can be most enhanced by incorporating behavioral finance into the client/adviser relationship. Once the adviser thoroughly understands the client and her motivations, the adviser knows what actions to perform, what information to provide, and the frequency of contact required to keep the client happy.

4. *Both client and adviser benefit from the relationship.* The primary benefit of incorporating behavioral finance into the client/advisor relationship is a closer bond between the two. This results in happier clients and an enhanced practice and career for the adviser.

Risk Tolerance Questionnaires

As one of the first steps in the client/adviser relationship, the adviser has the client fill out a risk tolerance questionnaire. Unfortunately, the same individuals can give different answers to the same set of questions depending on their frame of mind or current circumstances. In addition, most questionnaires are not structured to measure behavioral biases. This means there are a number of limitations to the traditional questionnaire.

First, since an individual's responses are affected by the wording of questions (framing), the same questions can produce different results if the structure of the questions is changed only slightly. Then, since client answers reflect all their behavioral biases, and those in turn are affected by the client's circumstances, administering a questionnaire only during the initial meeting is insufficient. Since the client's IPS should be analyzed annually for appropriateness, the questionnaire should also be administered annually.

Advisers also may interpret what the client says too literally, when client statements should only act as indicators. The successful adviser is able to determine the client's intent, for example, when he states a minimum allowable return in a given year. Rather than interpret the minimum allowable return literally, the adviser should use the statement as an indicator of the client's attitude toward risk and return. As a consequence, risk tolerance questionnaires are probably better suited to institutional investors, where less interpretation is required. Institutional investors are generally more pragmatic and tend to approach investing from a thinking/cognitive approach with a better understanding of risk and return.

BEHAVIORAL FACTORS AND PORTFOLIO CONSTRUCTION

LOS 7.c: Discuss how behavioral factors influence portfolio construction.

Research on defined contribution and 401k retirement plans in the U.S. indicates ways behavioral finance influences portfolio construction and how the insight gained might be applied in portfolio construction to achieve results more consistent with traditional finance theory. The studies show evidence of the following.

Status quo bias as investors do not make changes to their portfolio even when transaction costs are zero. Portfolio theory would clearly suggest that as time passes and the investors are aging, their optimal portfolio mix will shift. These changes are not being made. In addition, the investors generally accept whatever default investor option is offered by the employer and the contribution default rate. Neither is optimal as the asset mix is usually heavily weighted to money market funds and the contribution rate is lower than allowable.

To counteract this bias some companies have autopilot options such as target date funds. A target date fund has a stated retirement date and the manager of the fund automatically shifts the asset mix in ways suitable for investors planning to retire on that date. Once the investor picks the target date fund, the manager makes the adjustments for passage of time and the client does not need to take any action.

Naïve diversification as investors equally divide their funds among whatever group of funds is offered. According to a study, when offered a stock and bond fund, investors allocated 50/50. Then, if offered a stock and balanced fund, investors still allocated 50/50. Others suggest investors follow **conditional naïve diversification**. They select a smaller number of funds (e.g., three to five), and then allocate equally. In either case some argue this is motivated by seeking to avoid regret. Owning equal amounts of all, investors did not miss the best performer.

Excessive **concentration in employer stock** is also evident. This will be discussed in a later study session but it is very risky as retirement fund performance is now linked to compensation at an underlying source, the company. This could be based on *familiarity and overconfidence*. Employees may think, "I know the company and see it every day; surely it is a good investment." If past performance has been good and you are familiar with it that would be *naïve extrapolation of past results. Framing and status quo effect of* *matching contributions* is exhibited as if the employer's contribution is made in employer stock. In such cases the employees then increase the amount they chose to place in the employer stock. *Loyalty effect* is simply a desire to hold employer stock as a sign of loyalty to the company. When *financial incentives* are offer by the employer to invest in employer stock, the decision may be rational, but the holdings are in excess of what can be justified.

Excessive trading of holdings is evident in the brokerage account holdings of individuals even though individuals show status quo in retirement funds. This could be due to *overconfidence* as the individuals think they have superior stock selection skills or *self selection* as trading-oriented investors put their money in brokerage accounts and others put money in retirement portfolios at their company. Investors also show a *disposition effect* in selling stocks that appreciate (e.g., winners) but holding on to stocks that depreciate (e.g., losers).

Home bias is seen in under diversification and failing to invest outside the investor's home country.

LOS 7.d: Explain how behavioral finance can be applied to the process of portfolio construction.

Behavioral Portfolios vs. Mean Variance Portfolios

Investors exhibit behavioral biases when they construct portfolios in *layers*, comprising a pyramid with each layer having a specific purpose in achieving a different goal. This is also referred to as **mental accounting** because the assets in each layer of the pyramid are viewed separately from each other with no regard to how they are correlated.

In the pyramid structure, the most pressing goals are placed on the bottom layer and are met using low-risk, conservative investments. Each successive layer going toward the top of the pyramid is comprised of riskier assets to accomplish less immediate or less important goals. The top of the pyramid is comprised of risky, more speculative assets to meet "wish list" types of goals. Behavioral finance can be applied and benefit the portfolio management process by:

- Leading to the use of portfolios such as target funds, which work around the bias of investors to be static.
- Leading managers and clients to discuss the relative importance of goals and perceived risk. Tiered investment portfolios that the client can understand and maintain could be superior to traditional portfolios that consider correlation but that the client is unwilling to stay with.

ANALYST FORECASTS AND BEHAVIORAL FINANCE

LOS 7.e: Discuss how behavioral factors affect analyst forecasts and recommend remedial actions for analyst biases.

Research has shown that experts in varying fields make forecasting errors as a result of behavioral biases, and financial analysts are subject to those same biases. Surprisingly, it is analysts' superior skills in analyzing companies that makes them vulnerable to forecasting errors. An understanding of their weaknesses can help analysts limit the degree of their forecasting inaccuracies.

There are three primary behavioral biases that can affect analysts' forecasts: (1) overconfidence, (2) the way management presents information, and (3) biased research.

Overconfidence

Analysts can be susceptible to overconfidence as a result of undue faith in their own forecasting abilities caused by an inflated opinion of their own knowledge, ability, and access to information. Analysts also tend to remember their previous forecasts as being more accurate than they really were (a form of hindsight bias). As a result, they overestimate their accuracy and understate potential risk. There are several behavioral biases that contribute to overconfidence.

Analysts are subject to the *illusion of knowledge bias* when they think they are smarter than they are. This, in turn, makes them think their forecasts are more accurate than the evidence indicates. The illusion of knowledge is fueled when analysts collect a large amount of data. This leads them to think their forecasts are better because they have more and better information than others. Gathering additional information could add to an analyst's overconfidence without necessarily making the forecast more accurate. The *illusion of control bias* can lead analysts to feel they have all available data and have reduced or eliminated all risk in the forecasting model; hence, the link to overconfidence.

Exhibiting *representativeness*, an analyst judges the probability of a forecast being correct on how well the available data represent (i.e., fit) the outcome. The analyst incorrectly combines two probabilities: (1) the probability that the information fits a certain information category, and (2) the probability that the category of information fits the conclusion.

An analyst exhibits the *availability bias* when he gives undue weight to more recent, readily recalled data. Being able to quickly recall information makes the analyst more likely to "fit" it with new information and conclusions. The *representativeness* and *availability biases* are commonly exhibited in reactions to rare events.

To subconsciously protect their overconfidence, analysts utilize **ego defense mechanisms**. One ego defense mechanism is the *self-attribution bias.* Analysts take credit for their successes and blame others or external factors for failures. Self-attribution bias is an ego defense mechanism, because analysts use it to avoid the cognitive dissonance associated with having to admit making a mistake.

The relationship between self-attribution bias, illusion of knowledge, and overconfidence are fairly obvious. By aligning past successes with personal talent, the analyst adds to the feeling of complete knowledge, which in turns fuels overconfidence.

Hindsight bias is another ego defense mechanism. In effect, the analyst selectively recalls details of the forecast or reshapes it in such a way that it fits the outcome. In this way, the forecast, even though it technically was off target, serves to fuel the analyst's overconfidence. Hindsight bias then leads to future failures. By making their prior forecasts fit outcomes, analysts fail to properly recalibrate their models.

There are several actions analysts can take to minimize (mitigate) overconfidence in their forecasts. For example, they can self-calibrate better. *Self-calibration* is the process of remembering their previous forecasts more accurately in relation to how close the forecast was to the actual outcome. Getting prompt and immediate feedback through self evaluations, colleagues, and superiors, combined with a structure that rewards accuracy, should lead to better self-calibration. Analysts' forecasts should be unambiguous and detailed, which will help reduce hindsight bias.

To help counteract the effects of overconfidence, analysts should seek at least one counterargument, supported by evidence, for why their forecast may not be accurate. Analysts should also consider *sample size.* Basing forecasts on small samples can lead to unfounded confidence in unreliable models. Lastly, Bayes' formula is a useful tool for reducing behavioral biases when incorporating new information. Bayes' formula is discussed in the topic review, *The Behavioral Finance Perspective.*

Influence by Company Management

The way a company's management presents (frames) information can influence how analysts interpret it and include it in their forecasts. The problem stems from company managers being susceptible to behavioral biases themselves. There are three cognitive biases frequently seen when management reports company results: (1) framing, (2) anchoring and adjustment, and (3) availability.

Framing refers to a person's inclination to interpret the same information differently depending on how it is presented. We know, for example, that simply changing the order in which information is presented can change the recipient's interpretation of the information. In the case of company information, analysts should be aware that a typical management report presents accomplishments first.

Anchoring and adjustment refers to being "anchored" to a previous data point. Being influenced by (anchored to) the previous forecast, analysts are not able to fully incorporate or make an appropriate adjustment in their forecast to fully incorporate the effect of new information. The way the information is framed (presenting the company's accomplishments first), combined with anchoring (being overly influenced by the first information received), can lead to overemphasis of positive outcomes in forecasts.

Availability refers to the ease with which information is attained or recalled. The enthusiasm with which managers report operating results and accomplishments makes the information very easily recalled and, thus, more prominent in an analyst's mind. The more easily the information is recalled, the more emphasis (weight) it is given in the forecasting process.

Analysts should also look for **self-attribution bias** in management reports that is a direct result of the structures of management compensation packages. For example, management typically receives salary increases and bonuses based on operating results. Management is thus inclined to overstate results (overemphasize the positive), as well as the extent to which their personal actions influenced the operating results. Thus, self-attribution naturally leads to excessive optimism (overconfidence).

Analysts must also be wary of recalculated earnings, which do not necessarily incorporate accepted accounting methods. Again, since management compensation is based largely on operating results, there is a motivation to present the best possible data. The analyst should be particularly sensitive to earnings that are restated in a more favorable light than originally presented.

To help avoid the undue influence in management reports, analysts should focus on quantitative data that is verifiable and comparable rather than on subjective information provided by management. The analyst should also be certain the information is framed properly and recognize appropriate base rates (starting points for the data) so the data is properly calibrated.

Analyst Biases in Research

Biases specific to analysts performing research are usually related to the analysts' collecting too much information, which leads to the illusions of knowledge and control and to representativeness, all of which contribute to overconfidence. Two other common biases found in analysts' research are the *confirmation bias* and the *gambler's fallacy*.

The **confirmation bias** (related to *confirming evidence*) relates to the tendency to view new information as confirmation of an original forecast. It helps the analyst resolve cognitive dissonance by focusing on confirming information, ignoring contradictory information, or interpreting information in such a way that it conforms to the analyst's way of thinking. The confirmation bias can also be seen in analysts' forecasts where they associate a sound company with a safe investment, even though the stock price and the current economic environment would indicate otherwise.

The **gambler's fallacy**, in investing terms, is thinking that there will be a reversal to the long-term mean more frequently than actually happens. A *representative bias* is one in which the analyst inaccurately extrapolates past data into the future. An example of a representative bias would be classifying a firm as a growth firm based solely on previous high growth without considering other variables affecting the firm's future.

Professor's Note: The gambler's fallacy can be effectively demonstrated with a coin toss example. Consider an individual who is watching a coin being tossed. He knows intellectually that the probability of heads or tails turning up in any single toss is 50%. Before the coin is tossed the first time, he maintains this 50%/50% prior probability. Now, assume the coin is tossed five times, and heads turns up all five times. Knowing that the long-term mean is 50% heads and 50% tails, the individual starts to feel the probability of tails turning up on the next toss has increased above 50%. In fact, if the run of heads increases, the individual's subjective probability that tails will come up on the next toss will also increase, even though the probability of either heads or tails stays at 50% with every toss.

There are many actions an analyst can take to prevent biases in research, some of which are the same as when they are interpreting management reports. For example, analysts should be aware of the possibility of *anchoring and adjustment* when they recalibrate forecasts given new information. They should use metrics and ratios that allow for comparability to previous forecasts. They should take a systematic approach with prepared questions and gather data before forming any opinions or making any conclusions.

Analysts should use a structured process by incorporating new information sequentially and assigning probabilities using Bayes' formula to help avoid conclusions with unlikely scenarios. They should seek contradictory evidence, formulating a contradictory opinion instead of seeking more information that proves their initial hypothesis. They should get prompt feedback that allows them to re-evaluate their opinions and gain knowledge for future insight, all the while documenting the entire process.

INVESTMENT COMMITTEES

LOS 7.f: Discuss how behavioral factors affect investment committee decision making and recommend techniques for mitigating their effects.

Many investment decisions are made in a group setting (e.g., stock recommendations by research committees, analysts working in a team setting, pension plan decisions being approved by a board of trustees, or an investment club deciding which stocks to buy). The thinking is that the collective expertise of the individual members will contribute to better investment decision making. In a group setting, the individual biases mentioned before can be either diminished or amplified with additional biases being created.

Social proof bias is when a person follows the beliefs of a group. Research has shown that the investment decision making process in a group setting is notoriously poor. Committees do not learn from past experience because feedback from decisions is generally inaccurate and slow, so systematic biases are not identified.

The typical makeup of a committee coupled with group dynamics leads to the problems normally seen with committees. Committees are typically comprised of people with similar backgrounds and, thus, they approach problems in the same manner. In a group setting, individuals may feel uncomfortable expressing their opinion if it differs with others or a powerful member of the group. The remedy is for committees to have the following features:

- Comprised of individuals with diverse backgrounds.
- Members who are not afraid to express their opinions even if it differs from others.
- A committee chair who encourages members to speak out even if the member's views are contrary to the group's views.
- A mutual respect for all members of the group.

BEHAVIORAL FINANCE AND MARKET BEHAVIOR

LOS 7.g: Describe how behavioral biases of investors can lead to market characteristics that may not be explained by traditional finance.

In an efficient market, one should not be able to consistently generate excess returns using any form of information. Once information is known to investors, it should be instantaneously and fully incorporated into prices. But this does not mean that all apparent pricing exceptions to the efficient market hypothesis are anomalies.

- An excess return before fees and expenses that disappears after properly reflecting all costs required to exploit it is not an anomaly.
- Some apparent anomalies are simply a reflection of an inadequate pricing model. If another model with an additional risk factor removes the excess return, it may not be an anomaly.
- Apparent anomalies can just be small sample size. Just because flipping a coin three times generates three heads, does not make the odds on the next flip anything more than 50/50.
- An anomaly may exist for only the short-run and disappear once it becomes known and exploited.
- Some apparent anomalies are a rational reflection of relevant economic factors. Year-end trading anomalies may just reflect rational behavior to reduce taxes.

But other deviations from the EMH and rationality do persist and behavioral finance can offer insight into these.

Momentum Effect

All forms of the EMH assert technical-price-based trading rules should not add value. Yet studies continue to show evidence of correlation in price movement. A pattern of returns that is correlated with the recent past would be classified as a **momentum effect**. This effect can last up to two years, after which it generally reverses itself and becomes negatively correlated, with returns reverting to the mean. This effect is caused by investors following the lead of others, which at first is not considered to be irrational. The collective sum of those investors trading in the same direction results in irrational behavior, however. There are several forms of momentum that can take place, which are discussed in the following.

Herding is when investors trade in the same direction or in the same securities, and possibly even trade contrary to the information they have available to them. Herding sometimes makes investors feel more comfortable because they are trading with the consensus of a group. Two behavioral biases associated with herding are the *availability bias* (a.k.a. the *recency bias* or *recency effect*) and *fear of regret*. In the availability bias, recent information is given more importance because it is most vividly remembered. It is also referred to as the availability bias because it is based on data that are readily available, including small data samples or data that do not provide a complete picture. In the context of herding, the recent data or trend is extrapolated by investors into a forecast.

Regret is the feeling that an opportunity has passed by and is a *hindsight bias*. The investor looks back thinking they should have bought or sold a particular investment (note that in the availability bias, the investor most easily recalls the recent positive performance). Regret can lead investors to buy investments they wish they had purchased, which in turn fuels a **trend-chasing effect**. Chasing trends can lead to excessive trading, which in turn creates short-term trends.

Financial Bubbles and Crashes

Financial bubbles and subsequent crashes are periods of unusual positive or negative returns caused by panic buying and selling, neither of which is based on economic fundamentals. The buying (selling) is driven by investors believing the price of the asset will continue to go up (down). A bubble or crash is defined as an extended period of prices that are two standard deviations from the mean. A crash can also be characterized as a fall in asset prices of 30% or more over a period of several months, whereas bubbles usually take much longer to form.

Typically, in a bubble, the initial behavior is thought to be rational as investors trade according to economic changes or expectations. Later, the investors start to doubt the fundamental value of the underlying asset, at which point the behavior becomes irrational. Recent bubbles were seen in the technology bubble of 1999–2000 and increased residential housing prices in the United Kingdom, Australia, and the United States.

In bubbles, investors sometimes exhibit rational behavior—they know they are in a bubble but don't know where the peak of the bubble is. Or, there are no suitable alternative investments to get into, making it difficult to get out of the current investment. For investment managers, there could be performance or career incentives encouraging them to stay invested in the inflated asset class.

There are several different types of behavior that are evident during bubbles. Investors usually exhibit *overconfidence*, leading to excessive trading and underestimating the risk involved. Portfolios become concentrated, and investors reject contradictory information. Overconfidence is linked to the *confirmation bias*, in which investors look for evidence that confirms their beliefs and ignore evidence that contradicts their beliefs. *Self-attribution bias* is also present when investors take personal credit for the success of their trades (they make no attempt to link ex post performance to strategy).

Hindsight bias is present when the investor looks back at what happened and says, "I knew it all along." *Regret aversion* is present when an investor does not want to regret missing out on all the gains everyone else seems to be enjoying. The *disposition effect* is prevalent when investors are more willing to sell winners and hold onto losers, leading to the excessive trading of winning stocks.

As the bubble unwinds in the early stages, investors are anchored to their beliefs, causing them to under-react because they are unwilling to accept losses. As the unwinding continues, the disposition effect dominates as investors hold onto losing stocks in an effort to postpone regret.

Value vs. Growth

Two anomalies discussed by Fama and French[7] are associated with value and growth stocks. Value stocks have low price-to-earnings ratios, high book-to-market values, and low price-to-dividend ratios, with growth stocks having the opposite characteristics. In their 1998 study, Fama and French found that value stocks historically outperformed growth stocks in 12 of 13 markets over a 20-year period from 1975 to 1995. They also found that small-capitalization stocks outperformed large-caps in 11 of 16 markets. Additionally, they contend that in their three factor model, comprised of size, value, and market beta, the value stock mispricing anomaly disappears and is instead due to risk exposures of companies with a particular size and book-to-market value being more vulnerable during economic downturns.

Other studies have offered behavioral explanations, identifying the value and growth anomalies as a mispricing rather than an adjustment for risk. For example, in the **halo effect**, the investor transfers favorable company attributes into thinking that the stock is a good buy. A company with a good record of growth and share price performance is seen as a good investment with continued high expected returns. This is a form of representativeness in which investors extrapolate past performance into future expected returns, leading growth stocks to become overvalued.

The **home bias** anomaly is one where investors favor investing in their domestic country as compared to foreign countries. This also pertains to companies that are located closer to the investor. This bias can be related to a perceived information advantage or the comfort one feels from being closer to the home office or executives of the company. Analysts may see this as having easier access to those individuals, or a desire of the investor to invest in their community.

7. Fama, Eugene F. and Kenneth R. French, 1998. "Value versus Growth: The International Evidence." *Journal of Finance*, vol 53, no. 6: 1975-1999.

KEY CONCEPTS

LOS 7.a:
Incorporating behavioral biases into the client's IPS should result in the following:
- Portfolios that are closer to the efficient frontier.
- More satisfied clients.
- Clients who are better able to stay on track with their long-term strategic plans.
- Better working relationships between the client and adviser.

Limitations of classifying investors into behavioral types include the following:
- Individuals can display emotional and cognitive errors at the same time.
- The same individual may display traits of more than one behavioral investor type.
- As investors age, they become more risk averse and emotional toward investing.
- Individuals who fall into the same behavioral type shouldn't necessarily be treated the same.
- Unpredictably, individuals tend to act irrationally at different times.

LOS 7.b:
There are four areas of the client/adviser relationship that can be enhanced by incorporating behavioral finance into the relationship:
1. Behavioral finance helps the adviser understand the reasons for the client's goals.
2. Behavioral finance adds structure and professionalism to the relationship.
3. The adviser is better equipped to meet the client's expectations.
4. A closer bond between them results in happier clients and an enhanced practice for the adviser.

LOS 7.c:
Behavioral biases exhibited by defined contribution (DC) plan participants:
- *Status quo bias:* Investors make no changes to their initial asset allocation.
- *Naïve diversification (1/n naïve diversification):* Employees allocate an equal proportion of their retirements funds to each mutual fund in the plan.

Reasons employees invest in their own company's stock.
- *Familiarity:* They underestimate its risk; they become overconfident in their estimate of the company's performance.
- *Naïve extrapolation:* The company's recent good performance is extrapolated into expected future performance.
- *Framing:* If the employer's contribution is in company stock, employees tend to keep it rather than sell it and reallocate.
- *Loyalty:* Employees hold company stock in an effort to help the company (e.g., to prevent a takeover by another firm).
- *Financial incentive:* Tax incentives or the ability to purchase the stock at a discount lead to holding too much company stock.

Due to *overconfidence*, retail investors trade their brokerage accounts excessively. The result can be lower returns due to trading costs. *Disposition effect:* Investors tend to sell winners too soon and hold losers too long.

Home bias is closely related to *familiarity*. It leads to staying completely in or placing a high proportion of assets in the stocks of firms in their own country.

Mental accounting: Investors tend to construct portfolios in layers (pyramids). Each layer is used to meet a different goal. Investors see each layer as having a separate level of risk and ignore correlations of assets in the different layers.

LOS 7.d
Behavioral finance insights could lead to portfolio construction using:
- Target funds to overcome status quo bias.
- Layered portfolios that accommodate perceptions of risk and importance of goals to build portfolios the client will stay with.

LOS 7.e:
Analysts typically exhibit three biases: (1) overconfidence; (2) interpreting management reports; and (3) biases in their own research.

Behavioral biases that contribute to overconfidence:
- The illusion of knowledge bias.
- The self-attribution bias.
- Representativeness.
- The availability bias.
- The illusion of control bias.
- Hindsight bias.

Actions analysts can take to minimize overconfidence:
- Get feedback through self evaluations, colleagues, and superiors, combined with a structure that rewards accuracy, leading to better self-calibration.
- Develop forecasts that are unambiguous and detailed, which help to reduce hindsight bias.
- Provide one counterargument supported by evidence for why their forecast may not be accurate.
- Consider sample size and model complexity.
- Use Bayes' formula.

Reporting by company management is subject to behavioral biases:
- Framing.
- Anchoring and adjustment.
- Availability.

Analysts should be aware of the following when a management report is presented:
- Results and accomplishments are usually presented first, giving more importance to that information.
- Self-attribution bias in the reports.
- Excessive optimism.
- Recalculated earnings.

Actions the analyst can take to prevent undue influence in management reports:
- Focus on verifiable quantitative data.
- Be certain the information is framed properly.
- Recognize appropriate base rates so the data is properly calibrated.

Analyst biases in research:
- Usually related to collecting too much information.
- Leads to illusions of knowledge and control as well as representativeness.
- Inaccurately extrapolate past data into the future.
- Can suffer from *confirmation bias* and *gambler's fallacy*.

To prevent biases in research:
- Ensure previous forecasts are properly calibrated.
- Use metrics and ratios that allow comparability to previous forecasts.
- Take a systematic approach with prepared questions and gathering data first before making conclusions.
- Use a structured process; incorporate new information sequentially assigning probabilities using Bayes' formula.
- Seek contradictory evidence and opinions.

LOS 7.f:

Committee forecasts are usually no better than an individual's. In committees individual behavioral biases can be diminished or amplified. *Social proof bias* is when a person follows the beliefs of a group.

Committees are typically comprised of people with similar backgrounds; they tend to approach problems in the same manner. Individuals may feel uncomfortable expressing their opinions. To overcome these problems, construct committees with individuals who have diverse backgrounds, are not afraid to express their opinions, and have respect for the other members of the group.

LOS 7.g:

Market anomalies:
- *Momentum effect.* Patterns in returns that are caused by investors following the lead of others; they tend to trade in the same direction, which is referred to as *herding*.
- *Financial bubbles and crashes.* Periods of unusual positive or negative returns caused by panic buying or selling. They can be defined as a period of prices two standard deviations from their historical mean. A crash can also be characterized as a fall in asset prices of 30% or more over a period of several months; bubbles usually take much longer to form. Behavioral biases exhibited during bubbles are overconfidence, confirmation bias, self-attribution bias, hindsight bias, regret aversion, and the disposition effect.
- *Value stocks.* Low price-to-earnings, high book-to-market, low price-to-dividend ratios. Growth stocks have the opposite characteristics.

CONCEPT CHECKERS

1.   **Identify** three uses and three limitations of classifying investors into behavioral types.

2.   **List** and **explain** two areas that are considered critical to a successful client/adviser relationship and how incorporating behavioral finance can enhance the relationship.

3.   Which of the following is *least* indicative of the pyramid structure seen when individuals create portfolios?
        A. The correlation between the assets in the pyramid is ignored.
        B. Individuals subconsciously view the pyramid as having a single level of risk.
        C. People tend to place their money into different "buckets," which is referred to as mental accounting.

4.   Behavioral finance would support building portfolios using which of the following techniques?
        A. In a pyramid with low priority investment goals funded with low risk assets.
        B. In a balanced fund with stocks and bonds.
        C. Using target date funds.

5.   **Explain** why and how hindsight bias is used in an analyst forecasts.

6.   Which of the following is the *least* desirable trait to have in an investment committee?
      A. The committee members come from diverse backgrounds.
      B. The committee members are generally in consensus with one another.
      C. The chairperson of the committee encourages individuals to speak out.

7.   **Explain** what causes bubbles and crashes and **list** two ways of quantitatively identifying them.

For more questions related to this topic review, log in to your Schweser online account and launch SchweserPro™ QBank; and for video instruction covering each LOS in this topic review, log in to your Schweser online account and launch the OnDemand video lectures, if you have purchased these products..

ANSWERS – CONCEPT CHECKERS

1. Uses of classifying investors into behavioral types include:
   - Portfolios that are closer to the efficient frontier and more closely resemble ones based on traditional finance theory.
   - More trusting and satisfied clients.
   - Clients who are better able to stay on track with their long-term strategic plans.
   - Better overall working relationships between the client and adviser.

   Limitations of classifying investors into behavioral types include:
   - Individuals may display both emotional and cognitive errors at the same time, with either behavior appearing irrational.
   - The same individual may display traits of more than one behavioral investor type at the same time; therefore, the investment adviser should not try to classify the individual into only one behavioral investor type.
   - As investors age, they will most likely go through behavioral changes, usually resulting in decreased risk tolerance, along with becoming more emotional about their investing.
   - Even though two individuals may fall into the same behavioral investor type, each individual would not be treated the same due to their unique circumstances.
   - Individuals tend to act irrationally at different times, seemingly without predictability.

2. A successful client/adviser relationship can be defined in four areas, with each one being enhanced by an understanding of how behavioral finance can play an important part in the relationship.
   - The adviser understands the long-term financial goals of the client. Behavioral finance helps the adviser understand the reasons for the client's goals, making the client feel like they are better understood.
   - The adviser maintains a consistent approach with the client. Behavioral finance adds structure and professionalism to the relationship, which helps the adviser understand the client before investment advice is given.
   - The adviser invests as the client expects. Once the adviser understands the motivations for the client's goals, the adviser is better equipped to meet the client's expectations.
   - Both client and adviser benefit from the relationship. The primary benefit of incorporating behavioral finance into the client/advisor relationship is a closer bond between them, resulting in happier clients and an enhanced practice for the adviser.

3. **B** In the pyramid structure, investors view each separate layer or investment within that layer as having a separate level of risk associated with the goal they are trying to accomplish with that investment. It is in the traditional finance theory approach of portfolio construction where all the investor's assets are viewed as one complete portfolio with a single level of risk. In the pyramid structure, the correlation between the assets in the pyramid is ignored, whereas in the traditional finance portfolio construction, the correlation between the assets is taken into consideration. In the pyramid structure, individuals tend to think of each layer separately, which is referred to as mental accounting.

4. **C** Target date funds overcome the status quo bias of individuals and adjust the portfolio as they age. A simple balanced approach does not make the adjustment and a pyramid approach is suggested, but low priority goals can be funded with higher risk assets.

5. Hindsight bias is an ego defense mechanism analysts use to protect themselves against being wrong in their forecast. It is used by selectively recalling what actually happened, allowing the analyst to adjust their forecast accordingly and making it look like their forecast was more accurate than it actually was. Hindsight bias is possible when the original forecast is vague and ambiguous, a poor forecasting trait, allowing the forecast to be adjusted.

6. **B** Committee members always being in consensus with each other is an undesirable trait of a committee, which could lead to poor investment decision making. It is more desirable to have a committee comprised of individuals with diverse backgrounds who are encouraged, and not afraid, to voice their opinions, even if the opinion differs from the others. These traits lead to better overall decisions being made.

7. Financial bubbles and crashes are periods of unusual positive or negative returns *caused by panic buying and selling*, neither of which are based on economic fundamentals. In a bubble, the buying is due to investors believing the price of the asset will continue to go up. Another way of defining a bubble or crash is a period of prices for an asset class that is two standard deviations away from the price index's mean value. A crash can also be characterized as a fall in asset prices of 30% or more over a period of several months.

You have now finished the Behavioral Finance topic section. To get immediate feedback on how effective your study has been for this material, log in to your Schweser online account and take the self-test for this topic area. Questions are more exam-like than typical Concept Checkers or QBank questions; a score of less than 70% indicates that your study likely needs improvement. These tests are timed and allow three minutes per question.

INDEX

Notes

Notes

Notes

Notes

Notes

Notes

Notes

Notes

Notes

Notes

Notes

Notes

Notes

Notes

Notes

Notes